Triathlon For Youth

Dedication

Being passionate about triathlon can be trying on those around you, so it's important that I recognize some of the people who have provided so much support.

A big thanks to:

My wife Sharon, the ultimate role model, editor, wife and mom!

My parents, Ron and Mary Mackinnon, who provided me with so many incredible sporting and life opportunities that have shaped my life.

My in-laws, Val and Ian Adamson, who have been ever-encouraging.

Thomas Stengel, from Meyer and Meyer Publishing, who has been incredibly patient with me over the year this book took to develop, and has provided a magic touch that has got this book to print.

Finally, I have to thank my three amazing children, Chelsea, Sean and Ian, who make it all so worthwhile.

Ironman Edition

Triathlon for Youth

TRAINING

A HEALTHY INTRODUCTION TO COMPETITION

By Kevin Mackinnon

Published by Meyer & Meyer Sport

IRONMAN® is a registered trademark of World Triathlon Corporation

British Library Cataloguing in Publication Data
A catalogue record for this book is available from the British Library

Kevin Mackinnon
Triathlon For Youth
Oxford: Meyer & Meyer Sport (UK) Ltd., 2007
ISBN 10: 1-84126-110-6
ISBN 13: 978-1-84126-110-2

© 2007 by Meyer & Meyer Sport (UK) Ltd.
Aachen, Adelaide, Auckland, Budapest, Graz, Johannesburg,
New York, Olten (CH), Oxford, Singapore, Toronto
Member of the World
Sports Publishers' Association (WSPA)
www.w-s-p-a.org
Printed and bound by: B.O.S.S Druck und Medien GmbH, Germany
ISBN 10: 1-84126-110-6
ISBN 13: 978-1-84126-110-2
E-Mail: verlag@m-m-sports.com
www.m-m-sports.com

Contents

Preface

Children in today's society are in trouble. In Canada, 34 percent of children are considered clinically obese. The average child in North America spends about 28 hours watching television or playing computer games every week. (Yes, that's 4 hours a day!)

Those kids are growing up to become obese adults. Many of them aren't even making it to adulthood without serious health problems. Type 2 diabetes, a disease that affects overweight children, has become so common that many health professionals feel it has reached epidemic proportions here in North America.

It gets worse. We're now considered to be the first generation that is likely to see life expectancy actually drop ... in other words, kids today are not likely to live as long as we will.

While we have many children who are so inactive they are getting sick, we have another group of children at the other end of the sporting spectrum. These kids are being pushed into sports, and are doing too much, too soon.

Children should pursue a variety of sports while growing up. One of the worst things we can do as parents is force our children to specialize too soon. Seven-year-olds shouldn't have to give up every other sport to focus on hockey, and young teenagers shouldn't be giving up on their social lives and much of their scholastic careers in pursuit of the very, very slim chance that they might someday become a professional or elite athlete.

It's important to remember that our children aren't going to become great athletes just because we want them to become great athletes. As Dan and Jay Bielsma pointed out in their book, "So Your Son Wants to Play in the NHL," children make it in sports not because of what their parents do for them. Great athletes become the best at what they do because of their own inner drive to succeed.

This becomes even more apparent for young teenagers. There is a lot going on in their lives at this point. Any parent with a teenager will quickly tell you how important the social scene has suddenly become in their household! Then there's the whole issue of puberty ... a time where pre-teens and teenagers alike suddenly find themselves going through huge emotional and physical changes. There are lots of other things to do and worry about other than sports!

For the truly driven, though, nothing will get in the way. By the time I was 14, I would routinely spend six to eight hours a day on a tennis court during the summer. I dreamed of one day making it as a professional tennis player, but that was just part of my drive. I loved the challenge of what I was doing. I loved to see how far I could progress. While I loved to win, I also loved the journey and realization of all the hard work it took to get there.

This book does not offer any insight into how to become someone with that kind of drive. You either have that or you don't. What I do hope to provide in the following pages is some sort of a template that will help make it possible to enjoy pursuing excellence as an athlete. This book will show parents, and young adults, how they can strive to become as good as they can be in triathlon, a lifestyle sport that they will be able to pursue for the rest of their lives.

Introduction

"Don't let school get in the way of your education."

That's the way I start any talk that I have with teenage athletes. With the university athletes I work with, I have a completely different message: "Stay in school for as long as you can."

Sport should be the most enjoyable and educational activity we get to do growing up. It should provide teenagers (and almost teenagers) with a positive feeling about themselves. It should teach them that they can improve in all endeavors of life by working hard and persevering. It should teach them about the benefits of working as part of a team or training group. It should show them how much they gain in life by striving to achieve their goals. And, it should help them become good people.

Sounds a lot like the goals espoused by many schools, doesn't it? Over the last decade my wife and I have taken our children out of school for numerous extended trips, all because of sports. One year we were in Barbados for 10 days while I led a multinational children's training camp. Our children spent five days with 15 children from various Caribbean countries. They played games, they trained, they socialized, and they competed both as individuals and in a relay team. During that time, they got to chat and learn about the different cultures and traditions of the children who were attending.

Seen that happen in a classroom ... ever?

Last year the kids joined mom and dad for a two-week trip to Hawaii. The first week, they got to watch their parents compete in the World Aquathlon and Triathlon Championships. The second week was spent on the Big Island (Kona) where dad was covering the Ford Ironman World Championship. The highlight for my 12-year-old daughter? The wonderful conversation she had with Olympic Triathlon Champion Kate Allen from Austria, although chatting with two-time World Champion Michellie Jones was up there, too.

While my wife and I were acting as good role models, we were hardly the only ones that our kids could choose to emulate if they were to embark on a lifetime of triathlon fitness. The kids were all at the finish line when 80-year-old Robert McKeague and 75-year-old Sister Madonna Buder became the oldest man and woman to finish an Ironman race.

Those two trips are just a few of the ways that sports have allowed us to enhance our children's education, but traveling is only a small part of what makes athletic involvement so important in their lives.

Student athletes typically do better in school than their non-athletic peers. Athletics helps to develop healthy self-esteem and sense of self-confidence. During the often-challenging pre-teen and early-teenage years, sports can provide a positive, stable, and fun environment for youth who are going through all-too-many changes in their lives.

All of which is great, but there's a far more important reason that we need to keep these young athletes involved in sports between the ages of 12 and 16: their health. In addition to the recent studies that suggest this is the first generation that will see parents live longer

© 2004 - A Shot On Site

than their kids, childhood obesity has recently been dubbed an epidemic. Type 2 diabetes used to be known as "Adult Onset" diabetes until it became so prevalent in young children.

Many of the sports programs offered to younger children see huge declines in enrollment as the kids reach the teenage years. Thousands of young gymnasts and swimmers disappear from the gym and the pool once they hit high school. With all the other activities available to kids these days that don't involve physical activity, we're seeing the average teenager become an unhealthy and sedentary blob.

When I wrote "A Healthy Guide to Sport" two years ago, my goal was to motivate parents to get their children involved in an active lifestyle. In this book, I hope to continue that idea, but I'm hoping to get the message out to 12- to 16-year-olds who are looking toward a lifestyle filled with healthy competition.

Triathlon is just one of many "lifestyle" sports available to young athletes these days. Running, skiing, snowboarding, tennis, rollerblading, cycling, climbing ... the list could go on. All of these sports can be done for a lifetime, but I'd like to think that triathlon has something special that will make it a top pick for kids in the future.

The mixture of three sports, the panache of the worldwide venues, the ability to compete in the same arena as the best in the world ... all of these make triathlon a pretty exciting sport.

Which is all the more reason for kids to keep racing. This book will go a long way to making triathlon competition fun and rewarding.

Which brings me to why I tell the University students I coach to stay in school for as long as possible. Combining academic study with the pursuit of athletic excellence can be done. The national championship cross-country team that I competed on at university was filled with engineers, medical students, and accountants (I was the sole unemployable English student in the bunch!). During my university running career, athletics took me across Canada and the United States.

As a competitive runner, I was forced to be organized with my time. I quickly developed a routine that allowed me to keep a healthy balance between my athletic pursuits and my studies.

Some of the athletes I've coached have been able to use their athletic prowess to gain scholarships which have provided them expensive university education free of charge ... all the while experiencing the opportunities that high-level athletics provide.

None of which would be possible if they had stopped participating when they were 12 or 13 years old.

Note to Parents:

Throughout the book, I have tried to address myself to the young athletes I hope will find the information helpful. While I hope that many parents will also read the book, and learn from it, I figured it would be easier to try and speak directly to the young athletes this book is designed to help. (I'm hoping you parents will be understanding on that front!) Every now and again, though, I have a message that speaks directly to parents, which will be easy to identify ... those messages typically come under the title: Note to Parents ... just like this one!

CHAPTER 1

So You Want to Be a Champion?

Here's a question I like to put to kids who are involved in competitive sports programs:

What does it take to be a champion?

Is it talent? Strength? Enough money to provide the ultimate in coaching and equipment?

In all my years of coaching and being around world class triathletes, the two traits that seem to have defined any champions I have seen are dedication and perseverance.

Great athletes do what they do because of their own inner drive to succeed. Parents can't provide that. Coaches can't, either.

Here are a few more questions I like to pose to kids who are striving towards top-level athletics:

What position did Michael Jordan play for his high school team when he was in 9th grade? Actually, he didn't make the team.

How many goals did Wayne Gretzky score in the Brantford summer hockey league when he was 12? None. His father made him put his skates away for the summer to pursue other activities.

You don't need to become a world champion, or the greatest basketball or hockey player in history to justify pursuing an athletic career. While I managed to chalk up a few wins during my career as a professional triathlete, I hardly became a household name in the sport. Striving to become as good an athlete as I could be, though, has shaped my life.

If you are determined to see what you can achieve as an athlete, you have to compete. Competition can be a fantastic experience. It can also be a terrible one. The rest of this section will focus on competition, outlining the ways and approaches that will develop a healthy love of competition in young triathletes.

Why are you competing?

This is the first question you need to be able to answer if you have dreams of competing for a long time to come. I'll be honest ... at first, I didn't compete for the right reasons. While I loved to train, and was willing to put in all the time and training necessary to do well, mentally I was a wreck when it came to competing.

For the longest time in high school, competitors from other schools thought I was mute. That was because I used to get so nervous before a race that I couldn't talk. My best friend, Andrew MacNaughton, used to do all my communicating for me before races.

I still remember one cross-country running race that was coming down the wire. There was about 500 meters to go, and I was racing neck and neck with a boy who was a couple of years older than me. Desperate for some sort of motivation, I still remember telling myself that no one would like me if I didn't win.

I sure hope that wasn't true, but at the time it sure motivated me to get to the line first. While it worked that day, what would have happened to my psyche if I hadn't won?

While winning is lots of fun, I now know that there is much more to competition than simply getting to the finish line first. Grete Waitz, possibly the greatest marathon runner ever, was the first person I ever heard use the phrase, "It's all about the journey." At the time I didn't truly understand, but now I'm starting to get it. Athletics provided a great way to learn a lot about myself. My entire career is now based around triathlon, a sport that I pursued as a professional for eight years. While I never really made enough money through the sport to make a living, it did set me up for all the great things that have happened in my life since.

When you're 12, or when you're 16, none of that will seem to make much difference. You are likely competing because you're good at sports, or your friends are all doing them, or possibly your parents have insisted that you participate. I hope that you are also having fun! In the end, that's the most important reason to be involved. I also hope that while you are having fun, you will also begin to find out things about yourself that you didn't know, and develop traits that will take you a long way as an adult.

A positive environment

Wherever you're training, it should be a great place to be. Workouts should be fun, the coaches and athletes you're working with should be nice to be around and the general environment should be a good one. If it's not, you need to do something about it. Kids should talk to their parents, who can then talk to the coaches and administrators in hopes of making some changes.

Older teenagers should find themselves in a position where they can take things into their own hands and be able to communicate with their coaches directly. As a coach, I was thrilled when any of the athletes I worked with came to me with problems they were having with the group. It assured me that we had an open line of communication, and enabled me to stay on top of issues before they got out of hand.

How positive are you?

Want to hear one of the most important parts of being a champion?

Being a positive person yourself. Are you the kind of athlete coaches want to work with? Do you bring more to the training group than you take from it? Do your fellow athletes look to you for inspiration and leadership?

Every great athlete I have ever met displayed all of those traits. Sure, there have been some successful competitors who have been selfish, negative, and are no fun to be around. Very few of those people truly succeed in athletics, though, and even fewer are the kind of people others want to be around.

Ten tips to athletic success:

1 Set goals. Where do you want to take your athletics? Dream big, and don't be afraid to strive for the top.
2 Work Hard.
3 Be dedicated.
4 Don't let school get in the way of your education, but don't ever use sports as an excuse not to get one.
5 Be positive.
6 Be the kind of person who makes a difference.
7 Be a leader.
8 Be a good sport.
9 Be a good loser, but hate it.
10 Learn from your mistakes. A negative experience is only bad if you don't learn from it.

Six tips for athletic parenting success:

1 Be positive.
2 Be supportive.
3 Act as a role model.
4 Don't try to compete through your children.
5 Pay attention to what's going on!
6 Make sure sports remain fun.

Learning the hard way

When I was still competing, I used to swim with a competitive swim team. One of the kids who swam with the group, Mark Bates, was also a very talented triathlete, and as he was finishing high school, he asked me one day if I thought he should quit swimming in order to focus on his triathlon training.

I told him that based on what I saw of the future of the sport – at that time races did not allow drafting on the bike, but that seemed imminent to change as the sport tried to get accepted into the Olympics – he was better off to stick with swimming for a few more years until he had reached a national or international level. I felt that if he was going to be competitive at the Olympic level in triathlon, he was going to need that kind of swimming ability.

Mark didn't take my advice at that time. A few years later, he asked me to coach him, which I did for about five years. He would become a many-time national champion and finished as high as second at Ironman Canada during his incredibly successful career, but he wasn't able to reach one of his goals, qualifying for the Olympics.

While trying to qualify for the Olympic team in 1998, Mark was the one who reminded me of our swimming conversation from almost a decade before ... and acknowledged that part of the reason he didn't fare better in draft-legal races was because his swimming, while good, wasn't at a high enough level to compete in Olympic style events.

Mark's story is one I often recount when talking to parents about making sure their children compete in many different sports as they grow up. Competing at the highest levels in another sport, especially swimming, will only enhance a potential triathlon career.

It's important to expose yourself to as many different sporting opportunities as possible, especially if you have the opportunity to reach a competitive level with them! Don't become a "one-sport-wonders" too young – some of the world's greatest athletes grew up competing in many different sports before they pursued one sport exclusively.

Note to parents:

If I could, I would make you all read two books: "So Your Son Wants to Play in the NHL," by Dan and Jay Bylsma (Sleeping Bear Softwear, 1998), and "Raising A Good Sport in an In-Your-Face World: Seven Steps to Building Character on the Field – and Off," by George Selleck (Contemporary Books, Toronto, 2003).

The Bylsma's book offers the most complete look at the way parents and young athletes should approach sports by proving that ability is a tiny part of what makes a successful athlete. Athletes who succeed at the highest level get there because of their character. They don't give up. They respect themselves and their opponents. They learn from their mistakes, and their losses.

Successful athletes are, in two words, good sports, which is where George Selleck comes in. In "Raising a Good Sport" Selleck shows us what sport could and should be – not a mirror of our society, but a "beacon, pointing the way to a brighter future and a better world for our children and for generations of children to come."

Now before you turn the page in disgust at that lofty statement, bear with me for a paragraph or two. As I have said earlier in this book: sport should be the most enjoyable, and educational, activity our children get to do. It should provide them with a positive feeling about themselves. It should teach them that they can improve themselves in all endeavours of life by working hard and persevering. It should teach them about the benefits of working as part of a team. It should show them how much they gain in life by striving to achieve their goals. It should help them become good people.

That's what sports should do for our kids. More often than not, though, our children's sports experiences have none of those benefits. Typically they find themselves involved in events and races where the only thing that is emphasized is winning. They watch their coaches and parents yell and scream at referees and officials. If they aren't naturally gifted, they aren't provided adequate opportunities to improve their skills. Many of them spend their time training and racing trying to keep up, not doing so, and quitting.

Think about why your children are involved in sports. Make sure you're helping them enjoy a wonderful part of their future ... not pushing them towards a painful experience that will ultimately see them give up.

CHAPTER 2

Training: How Much?

Training should be fun. Except for the lucky few who can actually make a living as professional triathletes, triathlon is something adults and teenagers do because they enjoy it, like to compete, like the feeling of accomplishment after finishing a race, enjoy the health and physical benefits of being involved in three sports ... well, there are likely a lot more reasons, hopefully those will do as illustration!

The "fun factor" is important, but the stress of trying to fit enough training into a busy schedule can often overwhelm people. It is very easy to become completely engrossed in the sport, regardless of age. Adults will get to the point where much of the rest of their lives gets forgotten as they pursue their sport. The same can happen to young teenagers. Suddenly trying to excel in three different sports can become an all-encompassing reason to give up other sports, music, or friends.

It's important that young athletes try to maintain as much of an all-rounded approach to their lives as they can. There is plenty of time to pursue an athletic career, but you only get to grow up once. It is a shame to pass up on the many opportunities available in high school because of a warped focus on the sport.

Quality and consistency

There are many youth programs that push young adults at too high a level. My son was burnt out of a competitive gymnastics program that had him training 10-hours-a-week when he was just nine. I still remember arguing with my own swim coach as a 24-year-old professional when I tried to suggest that the girls half my age who were training in my lane shouldn't be swimming more in a week than I was running.

If there is one thing you take from this book, it is this:
It isn't how much training you do that will make the difference, it is the quality of your training that will get you to the finish line as fast as you want to and help you develop as an athlete. The most important aspect of your training is consistency. Some very successful athletes have managed to make themselves competitive on just a few workouts a week.

Consistency
What does consistency mean? Endurance sports like triathlon differ from other sports in that there isn't really a training "season" and "off-

season." I remember in high school looking on enviously as the hockey and football players simply stopped training for a good portion of the year, enjoying their "off-season" break with gusto while I, the distance runner, had to maintain my training regimen throughout the year.

By the time a young endurance athlete reaches the age of 12, they can start to build a base of training. That doesn't mean you need to be training a lot – I've outlined some general guidelines of what might be an appropriate level and number of hours of training later in this chapter.

Some of the top athletes I have worked with have taken more than a year to get to the point where I felt they were ready to train. If you are a 12-year-old athlete just taking up the sport, your goal should be to gradually build to the point where you can do some serious training ... when you're 18! Remember where you're going. It is important not to do too much, too early. If you try to put in 20 hours of training every week when at 12, how much will you/ should you be doing at 18?

Burn out

There's an even more important aspect to the concept of consistency: making sure you don't burn out. Do you want to be remembered for the great race you had when you were 12, or the Olympic Games you attended when you were 20?

There is a huge drop off in participation in many sports as children reach high school. With a myriad of other activities available to them, the desire to be more social and hang out with friends and the pressures of school, sports may become less "fun" for young athletes. (None of those factors take into consideration the many physical changes teenagers are experiencing as they reach puberty, too.)

All of those factors aside, over trained teenagers are more likely to quit their sport than those for whom it continues to be a fun activity. It comes back to this simple point: if you push too hard, too early, there is a good chance that you're going to be out of the sport before you reach your true potential.

So what is appropriate?

It's amazing what people can endure before things fall apart. As a 17-year-old runner, I ran 105 high intensity miles (almost 170km) a week for almost three months before my body gave in. I developed tendonitis in my hip that forced me to stop running for months.

Even experienced parents can be deceived. My wife and I reluctantly allowed our nine-year-old son to become involved in a competitive gymnastics program a few years ago. It wasn't long before he was training 10 hours a week, a training load that we, as parents, both felt was too much, but since he remained keen to head off to practice four days a week, we allowed him to continue.

Not even a year into the program we found ourselves at the local hospital with a young boy who was suffering from a severe case of pneumonia. His resistance at an all-time low, he was sick for months. We learned the hard way that it's best to stick with your "gut" when it comes to evaluating your child's workload when dealing with training!

So what's the right amount of training? Good question ... and as soon as I figure out a magic number, I'll write another book on that alone!

Each individual will be able to handle different amounts of training. A good coach will be able to monitor the workload of each of his or her athletes accordingly. It's also important that the program you're involved in builds training gradually both through the year, and year-by-year. If the 12-year-olds in a competitive swim program are swimming 6,000 to 8,000 meters a week, the 13-year-olds should be swimming 10,000 to 12,000 meters every week, for example. Even that is a huge jump – about a third more distance a week over a one-year period, but often you'll see programs where the kids will literally double their mileage from one year to the next.

In terms of week-to-week build-ups, the common coaching philosophy is that you should never increase training volume by more than 10 percent. This is an important process to remember when first starting out in a program, no matter what the sport. Increasing the training volume too much, too soon, can lead to injury and overtraining.

Racing and training volumes

Here are the Canadian race distances for athletes between the ages of 12 and 16:

Age Division	12 to 13	14 to 15	16 to 19
Maximum Distances	300m / 15km / 3km	500m / 15km / 4km	750m / 20km / 5km

In the U.S., the distances for 12- to 15-year-olds are shorter: 200m swim / 10k bike / 2k run.

With that in mind, any triathlon training program should be geared toward those distances. If a 12-year-old has to run 3km in a race, does it make sense to have them competing in 10km running races? In fact, based on the race distances above, it doesn't even make sense to have a 16-year-old running that far in races.

So why do so many junior triathlon programs seem to push young athletes to swim, bike and run much further than they have to race? I'm not sure. Part of the answer likely lies in the fact that it's easy to see results when you have people simply trying to go further and further. It's easy to see an improvement when you can say that one month Junior ran 3km, and the next he ran four.

It's much harder to get faster, which ultimately should be the goal for young triathletes. As the distances show, junior triathlon events aren't particularly long. To do well requires talent, technique and speed. It is these components of a youth triathlon training program that will produce the optimal results. What should the optimal results of a triathlon program be? In my opinion, a good program should keep kids in the program, see them improve year by year, and develop successful and competitive junior triathletes!

Doing too much, too soon, won't achieve those results.

Is there a formula of how much a 12-year-old should be doing? Unfortunately, there is not. Different children will develop at different levels. What I can say, though, is that it's important to remember where the program is going. As you will see in the training section later, I believe that 12- to 14-year-olds should aim for no more than six workouts a week. Those workouts should be about 60 to 90 minutes long (not all should be 90 minutes − that would be nine hours of training a week, which is likely too much!), and incorporate lots of technique, flexibility ... and fun!

CHAPTER 3

Types of Training

Every training program requires a few basic components. These types of training need to be emphasized a bit more at certain times of the year, and less than others, but should all be included in any training program.

Each type of training works on a different aspect of fitness. A successful competitor will have to be relatively proficient in each area. In the training process, I focus on four different training parameters. Some coaches will include many more – I used to work with a swim coach who created programs based on seven different training systems – but I have always found that the KISS (Keep It Simple, Stupid!) approach to training always works best. Consistent athletes who incorporate these four types of training in their programs routinely excel.

So, does that mean that as a 12-year-old you need to make sure that your training program is elaborate enough to include all of these types of training? No! Incorporating some of this training into a pre-teen's program is a great start, one which will pay great dividends when they reach the age of 15 or 16. Older athletes, though, should begin to pay attention to their training, and begin to try and understand the goal of specific workout sessions.

Here's a short breakdown on each of the four types of training (and strength training) that I will provide workouts for in each of the specific sport sections:

Distance (Aerobic) training

(60-80% effort)
Basically, this type of training helps you to ensure that you're going to be able to go the distance. These are easy workouts designed to improve your basic cardiovascular system, and to train your body to burn fat, the most efficient energy source.

Your body burns fat when there's enough oxygen in the system. In other words, you have to be able to breathe relatively effortlessly! The easiest way to ensure that you training aerobically, or doing a proper distance effort, is to try the talk test while you're doing these types of workouts. You have to chat with your buddies while you're doing your distance training! If you're too out of breath to keep up a conversation, you're going too hard!

These sessions typically last 20 minutes or longer. This type of training should be emphasized during the early season, but should be maintained at some level throughout the year as your easy training sessions.

Strength training

These workouts are designed to help you develop some strength and power. On the bike, these will be either harder sessions on the wind trainer, or hills. For running, these will be stair and hill sessions.

VO$_2$ Max training

(80-90% effort)

Your VO$_2$ refers to the "volume of oxygen." During a VO$_2$ Max test, the goal is to measure the volume of oxygen per minute per kilogram of body weight. (Have I lost you yet?) In simple terms, the VO$_2$ Max test measures how good your body is at getting oxygen around to the muscles.

VO$_2$ max intervals are hard efforts with a fairly good recovery. Typically, VO$_2$ Max intervals are between three and eight minutes long, and require a half to full recovery. So, if you were doing three minute intervals, you would need to recover for at least 1$^{1}/_{2}$ minutes, and you could take as long as three minutes to recovery before starting the next interval.

These sessions should be a mainstay of your training towards the beginning of the race season. You should try to do one VO$_2$ Max set of intervals in each sport, every week, to help maintain your cardiovascular efficiency.

Anaerobic threshold training

(75-85% effort)

Your anaerobic threshold (AT) is the point at which your body ceases to work aerobically and starts to produce lactic acid. Basically, this is the gauge of how efficient your body is when racing – how hard you can push before your body will have to slow down.

These are hard intervals with a very short recovery. The idea during these sets is to never completely recovery before you start the next interval. While it might seem and sound like torture, these can be fun sets!

AT intervals should be 30 seconds to three minutes long, although you'll see in some of the workouts I've included in the various programs that there are some AT interval sessions where the intervals are only 15 seconds long. I've seen many of the young athletes I coach excel coming off of those shorter AT sets, which is why I like to incorporate them into the training plan.

These intervals should be maintained in your training throughout your competitive training season, but become important once you start racing.

Sprint training

(90-100% effort)

How fast are you? Can you out-sprint the rest of the school, or are you one of those folks who doesn't have the speed that the rest of the class has, but can go all day?

If you want to race faster, you have to be faster. Let's say you wanted to set a new record at the school for the 1,500 meter race. To get the record, you need to run the $3^3/_4$ laps of a 400 meter track in five minutes. That works out to 80 seconds per lap. If your best time for 400 meters is 78 seconds, there is no way you're going to average two seconds slower for almost four laps!

So, if you really want that record, there's no point training yourself to run longer distances at a slow pace. You need to get fast! This is where sprint training comes in. These are short intervals of anywhere from 15 seconds to a minute, with lots of recovery. (You want to feel completely rested before you start the next interval.)

Triathletes often shy away from these types of interval sets, but they really shouldn't. No matter what level you are competing at, the faster you are, the easier the pace will feel. So, if you're running along with a pack of your competitors, and you're the fastest in the group, the pace will feel much easier to you than it will for your competition!

Sprint training intervals should also be incorporated almost throughout the competitive training period, but become really important over the last few weeks of the season or when you're trying to get ready for a big race.

What to emphasize, when

For most people in North America, the triathlon race season takes place between June and August. With that in mind, here's an example of how you might structure the types of training you are doing each week from February to the end of the season.

- **February:** The majority of your workouts should be distance sets.
- **March:** About half of your workouts should be distance sets. Now you should add one workout a week of intervals and strength, which should include some hills (run) and VO_2 Max intervals.

- **April:** About one third of your workouts should be distance sets. If you do three workouts in each sport each week, one session should be a strength session of hills or harder riding on a wind trainer. Another session should be a set of VO_2 Max and AT intervals or fartlek.
- **May:** About one quarter of your workouts should be distance oriented, with another session of strength and VO_2 Max intervals, and another of AT and Speed Training intervals.
- **June:** About one quarter of your workouts should be distance oriented, with another session of AT and VO_2 Max intervals, and another of AT and Speed Training intervals.
- **July and August:** About one quarter of your workouts should be distance oriented, with another session of AT and Speed Training intervals, and another of AT and Speed Training intervals.

Note: Many of the workouts you will find included at the end of each specific sport section are not meant to be complete workouts – I have created a number of shorter "sets" so that you can combine them to fit into the above patterns.

CHAPTER 4

Rest

In keeping with the endurance, type-A, more-is-better "personality" that tends to be drawn toward triathlon, even young teenagers will tend to push themselves too hard. Most endurance athletes don't rest enough. It's important to build rest into every training program. So important, in fact, that rest should be the first component of the training plan to be incorporated in the training schedule.

The day off

The first step in that process is to plan a day off every week. One day when there is absolutely no athletic activity. That doesn't mean an easy swim, a light run, an easy bike. It means a day completely off from any structured sports activity.

Does that mean a 14-year-old couldn't head off to the basketball court on that day? Sure they can. Playing with their friends, having fun doing something other than swimming, biking and running can provide a wonderful mental and physical break.

The structured day off can also be a great day for family to spend some time together. Through the winter, it might be a family ski day on the weekend. In the summer, a fun option might be to enjoy a night away to do some camping.

Whatever the age, or competitive level, it's critical that there is one day off every week. As an athlete, I like to have Friday as my day off. After a long week of school, or work, it was nice not to feel any pressure to get out and do a workout.

Helping to taper

Once race season hits, there's an even more important reason to have Friday as a day off.

More than a decade ago, in a study done at McMaster University on peaking, it was found that athletes who did some activity the day before a race did better than those who rested completely the day before the competition. (There's more on that study in the chapter on pre-race preparation and peaking.) The study seemed to indicate that unless the muscle fibers were forced to work, they wouldn't store any glycogen.

In basic terms, muscles seem to store more energy when they are worked the day before the race, not rested. It is important, though, to rest before a competition, which is why it is best to rest two days before the race.

Younger athletes will benefit from more than one day off a week. When first getting involved in the sport, two or three days off every week will likely help ensure these young athletes don't overdo things, and have fun with their activity.

Tired? Don't be afraid to rest

No matter what the age, if athletes are feeling tired they should listen to their body and either back off the training intensity or volume, or rest completely. If rest is an integral part of the training schedule, there is less chance that those "bad" or tired days will occur.

CHAPTER 5

Setting up a Training Program

One of the hardest parts of organizing your triathlon training is figuring out how to schedule everything. When I first started in the sport, there were no coaches around to help me put together a training schedule, so I did my own thing. I was serious about my training, and, since I had been running almost twice a day for eight years, I figured that if I was going to be a serious triathlete, I should try to swim, bike and run every day. Needless to say, I managed to completely over train, and spent a lot of time completely exhausted!

The one thing I did do right, though, was to make sure I took a day off every week. That's the first thing to work into your training program. After that, the next thing you need to figure out is what days you need to hook up with a group. For example, my children meet with a track group for an hour on Tuesday and Thursday nights, followed by a 45 minute swim with a swim group those same evenings. (An example of their program appears in the "advanced" competitor program below.)

The programs below are just examples of training plans that you might want to try and use – feel free to modify them as best fit your training time and commitments.

When first starting out, it's probably realistic to aim for one workout a day, with two days off every week to pursue other activities.

Here's a sample schedule for a beginner:
- Monday: off
- Tuesday: Swim
- Wednesday: Bike
- Thursday: Run
- Friday: Off
- Saturday: Swim
- Sunday: Bike/ Run Transition workout

A more advanced competitor can add another couple of workouts to the program:
- Monday: off
- Tuesday: Swim (intervals)/ Run (easy)
- Wednesday: Bike (intervals)
- Thursday: Swim (easy)/ Run (intervals)
- Friday: Off
- Saturday: Swim (intervals)/ Bike (easy)
- Sunday: Bike/ Run Transition workout

Another way to fit those workouts in a week might look like this:
- Monday: Run (easy)
- Tuesday: Swim (intervals)
- Wednesday: Bike (intervals)
- Thursday: Swim (easy)/ Run (intervals)
- Friday: Off
- Saturday: Swim (intervals)/ Bike (easy)
- Sunday: Bike/ Run Transition workout

Athletes involved in a competitive program might be required to attend more practices in one sport. This will be especially true in swimming. If that's the case, drop a bike and run workout every week, and try to get in a few short workouts on your bike or out running around your swim training.

- Monday: Swim
- Tuesday: Swim/ Bike (intervals)
- Wednesday: Swim
- Thursday: Swim/ Run (intervals)
- Friday: Off
- Saturday: Swim/ Bike (easy)
- Sunday: Bike/ Run Transition workout

As you can see, the options are endless when it comes to setting up a training program. Keep a few things in mind when it comes to organizing your training:

- Make sure to have a complete day off every week
- Do your best to avoid two hard days in a row
- If you're participating in a competitive program (swimming or running most commonly), don't try and maintain the same level in all three sports. You'll be getting a fair amount of general fitness from your main sport, so you won't need to do as much training in the other sports to maintain fitness in them.

CHAPTER 6

Swimming

Equipment

The equipment needs for swimming are fairly basic: goggles, a swim suit, and a bathing cap.

Goggles

Many different companies make a variety of styles of goggles, so finding a comfortable pair that fit properly (read, don't leak!) can be done. That's easy enough to say, I know, and I have seen how difficult it is to put into practice.

One of the keys to finding the right pair of goggles is to go to a store that offers a large selection. Try on a few different styles and brands until you come up with a pair that works.

A trick we have found to help in the Mackinnon household is to put the goggles on without using the straps. If you can generate a seal and enough suction to keep the goggles on your face without falling off, there's a good chance you have found a good-fitting pair.

Over the last few years, "mask-style" goggles have become available and provide a lot of underwater vision, which is especially appreciated during open water swims. These goggles, while comfortable, aren't particularly suited for pool racing, so if you are going to be taking part in any swimming races, you might want to look for a different style.

Swim suits

As you become more competitive and interested in the sport, you'll want to get a more specialized suit.

"Speedo-style" suits are the norm in this regard. Made either of nylon or of a lycra/ nylon blend, the suits should be snug fitting to reduce drag in the water. Nylon suits aren't as comfortable, but stand up to the rigors of chlorinated pools much better than suits with more lycra in them.

For racing, you can get some really high-tech suits made of water repellent material. These suits typically come with a high price tag, so you'll definitely need to be serious about your swimming before you, or your parents, invest in one of these.

Bathing caps

Caps are usually made of latex, but there are caps made of both silicon and neoprene, too. Caps are typically supplied at races, and

should be worn whenever you're swimming in open water as you will be easier to see with one on. Since so much heat is lost through the head, a cap will also help you stay warm in colder water.

Wetsuits

Swimming in colder water is considerably more comfortable with a wetsuit. If you're still growing, this is not likely a great investment until you're older, and have to swim longer distances in cold water.

Wetsuit background

When Mark Montgomery was asked by two-time Ironman finisher Dan Empfield to try out a wetsuit in 1986, he was a bit skeptical. At that time in North America, wetsuits were worn by triathletes only in the most extreme conditions. There weren't any high-tech suits designed specifically for swimming back in the dark-ages of the sport. Pros, me included, wore ill-fitting surfing suits when faced with cold water conditions. Montgomery wasn't optimistic that Empfield's suit would make much of a difference to his swim times.

After 500 m, though, Montgomery climbed out of the pool, and assured Empfield that within two months he'd have every pro on the west coast in a suit. He did that, and more. Within three months he had pros from around the world in one of Empfield's Quintana Roo suits, including yours truly.

What was it that made Empfield's suit so special? Instead of a suit designed for surfing, this smooth, buoyant and tight-fitting suit was specifically designed for swimming. Empfield experimented with various thicknesses of rubber, too, eventually determining that 5 mm thick neoprene provided the optimal results.

Things have changed dramatically over the last 20 years. Now there are a number of companies, including Blue Seventy, the makers of the Ironman Wetsuits, that offer wetsuits in various styles that will differ based on fit, thickness, and sleeves.

Generally, full suits are faster than sleeveless suits. If you live in a country where you're likely to be swimming in colder water, you're best to pick a full suit: the extra warmth it will provide, especially during those cold, early season races will be much appreciated!

Unless you've stopped growing, I wouldn't suggest running out to buy the most expensive wetsuit out there. Those suits can be very expensive, and for the distances you should be swimming, the advantages those suits provide aren't likely to make enough of a difference to warrant the cost.

The most important factor when getting a wetsuit is fit. Make sure you get your suit from a store where they take the time to have you try the suit on, and make sure it's the right size, style and cut for you.

Training tools

Many swim programs will utilize training tools like pull buoys, kick boards, paddles and fins. As you get more serious about your triathlon training, your swim coach might suggest that you invest in some or all of these so that you have ready access to them for training. Here's what these tools are all about:

Pull buoys

Placed between your legs, pull buoys allow you to swim without kicking. This can be particularly helpful for developing the "roll" in your stroke. (See the section on freestyle later in this chapter.) They are also a useful tool for helping you get a feel for how you'll feel swimming in a wetsuit – your legs will be higher in the water and you'll have to kick less.

Paddles

Often used in conjunction with pull buoys, paddles can help you develop some strength and enhance proper technique. These do require a fair amount of strength, so aren't really a tool that should be utilized until you're well into your teens.

Kick boards

An important part of your swim stroke is your kick, which is why your swim coach is likely to have you doing a fair amount of kicking using a board. Most pools have an abundance of boards, but some swim programs might require you to have your own if they meet at a pool that doesn't have them.

Fins

These are also often used in conjunction with a kick board. Fins help develop your kick, and can also help work on your ankle flexibility.

Note for parents:

What to look for in a swim program

If you do end up signing your child up on a team, make sure you do your homework before you sign on the dotted line.

Swim programs are notoriously demanding on both children and parents. Two-a-day workouts can quickly become the norm. At one point in my triathlon career, I swam with an age group team, and worked with a group of young teenagers in what we called the "distance" lane.

One 13-year-old I swam with often swam 80 kilometers in a week! To this day I find it crazy that this girl was swimming as much as I was running every week … and I was making a living from my training!

Before you get involved with a swim program, talk to the coaches, and some of the parents who have children in the program. Take in a few of the practices.

Are the kids having fun? Are the coaches supportive? Do they stress the long-term development of the athlete?

Look for a program that emphasizes quality training and skill development over extreme distance training. Kids who intend to focus on triathlon shouldn't be swimming every day, either.

Swimming skills

The basic stroke used in triathlons is "freestyle," or "front crawl." One arm extends in front of the body. The hand enters the water first – leading with the fingers. Once the hand has entered, the arm continues to extend for a short time before pulling under the water. During that short extension the shoulders roll. As you become more proficient with your stroke, it's important to try and have your hips roll in conjunction with your shoulders to create the optimal body position through the water. The entire body should roll – other than the head, which stays in a fairly straight position, with the water level kept just above the level of your swim goggles.

Once the arm is fully extended, it starts to pull under the water. It's important that your hand remain under your body throughout the pulling section of the stroke. The hand, as it is pulling under the water, makes a very gradual "S" shape as it makes a slight "outsweep" followed by a move inwards, and finished with another "outsweep" motion to finish the stroke. It's important to remember that the hand shouldn't ever cross the mid-line of the body. The elbow shouldn't bend too much, either, during this pulling phase – depending on how strong you are, the bend in the elbow during this part of the stroke will be anywhere from 45- to 90-degrees.

After sweeping away from the body to finish the stroke, the arm recovers. The more the athlete rolls, the easier this recovery phase will be, as the shoulder will be further out of the water. The elbow should be fairly high during this phase, and the forearm and wrist should be very relaxed and loose.

Here are some coaching tips that will help you with your front crawl:

Head position

The head should be in a relaxed position looking at the bottom of the pool. The water line should be at about the hairline, or swim-cap line. The head should remain in that position unless a breath is taken.

If the head is up too high, your hips and legs will tend to sink. The goal is to have the head in a position that makes it easy for your back, hips and legs to be flat, and relatively close to the top of the water.

Breathing

One of the hardest parts of the freestyle stroke is coordinating the breathing action. The head should rotate along with the shoulders when taking a breath. Hopefully you were taught to "bilaterally" breathe, meaning that you breathe on alternate sides, which is very useful and important because it promotes a more balanced stroke. If you aren't comfortable with bilateral breathing ... get practicing! It will make a big difference in your swimming.

Hand entry

Must be at shoulder width, with the fingers entering first. You were likely originally taught to enter with your thumb first. As you get older, and more competitive, you will find that by having your fingers enter first, you'll be able to generate more power with your stroke, and you will be more likely to pull underneath your body.

If your hands are entering within the shoulders, you'll most likely develop a "fishtail-type" motion through the water, rather than the desired rolling motion. If your hands are entering wider than your shoulders, your shoulders will be doing most of the work pulling you through the water, not the large muscles in your back.

Arm bend

As the arm pulls under the water, the arm should not bend too much. The elbow remains "high" in this position – it should be above the hand as the arm pulls through the water. Don't emphasize the "S" part of the stroke too much other than to promote the out-to-in-to-out aspect of the pulling motion.

Recovery

It's important that the arm be relaxed and bent during the recovery phase. The elbow should be fairly high out of the water.

Kicking

It's important to kick from the hips, as opposed to bending the knees too much. (If you kick from the knees, you can actually generate more of a backwards force than a frontward force!) It's also important to make the kicking motion more of a downward action as opposed to upwards.

Triathletes shouldn't over kick – the idea is to kick just enough to keep the legs up, but not so much that the legs will be tired for the bike and run portions of the event!

With that in mind, the ideal kick for young triathlete to learn is what we call a "two-beat" kick: the right leg kicks downwards as the left arm enters the water, and the left leg kicks downwards as the right arm enters the water.

Head up strokes

It's important during open water swims to be able to sight by doing a head up stroke. This requires an extra push down on the water as the arm extends in order to bring the head right up and out of the water in order to be able to look ahead.

Swim workouts

Distance:

300m to 1000m straight swim. This can be broken up by changing strokes along the way, or by changing speeds (i.e. 25m hard/ 25m easy) along the way.

VO$_2$ Max:

2-5 x 200m/1-2 MRI (minutes rest interval)

4-8 x 150m/ 45-60 SRI (seconds rest interval)

AT:

4-8 x 100 m/ 15-30 SRI

4-12 x 75 m/ 10-30 SRI

4 x {4 x 50/ 5 SRI} 1 MRI/ sets

This set would mean doing four intervals of 50m, taking a break of 5 seconds between each one, and taking an extra minute after the fourth interval

Sprint Training:

4-8 x 100 m/ 1-1:30 RI

6-12 x 50 m/ 30-60 SRI

2 x 200 m/ 2 MRI

CHAPTER 7

Biking

Equipment

First things first:
Don't ride without a helmet!

The most important piece of equipment for biking, other than the bike, is a helmet. It must be an approved helmet – in North America that means that it meets either ANSI (American National Standards Institute) or Snell standards.

It's also critical the helmet fits properly. It should be the correct size – there shouldn't be too much movement from side to side or front to back, and the straps should be adjusted properly.

The "V" of the strap on the side of the helmet should be just below the ear. You shouldn't be able to get more than two fingers between the chin strap and neck.

Bikes

When first getting involved in triathlon, regardless of age, I always encourage people to start with whatever bike they already have. There is no point investing in an expensive road or triathlon bicycle for your first race – make sure you're going to get involved, and stay involved before you make any big investments.

Most young athletes will likely get started using a mountain bike as this is the most common bike people will have in their garage or basement. While a mountain bike will get the job done, it will do it at a much slower pace than the bikes the fast-moving speedsters use who may also be entered in the race. Once you're competing in events for those 12 years and older, there are likely going to be more than a few of those fast moving road bikes in the transition area.

If participation is your only goal, ignore the rest of this section! The mountain bike that you have will get you through the race, you'll have fun, you'll have less of a chance of getting a flat and you'll be able to ride through the trails back to the parking lot!

Those who intend to take things a bit more seriously will want to look into a road or triathlon bike. One trip to the local bike store will no-doubt convince you of two things: there are lots of options available and trying to decide between them can be quite difficult. (I should probably have added one other part of that piece – many of the options can be very expensive!)

It is important, though, that whatever bike you end up getting fits you properly. This is where a trip to a reputable bike store makes all the difference. If you are fit on the bike properly, you shouldn't be too stretched out reaching for the handlebars (your elbows should be bent only slightly), and when your foot is on the pedal at the bottom (in line with the seat tube), your knee should only be slightly bent.

Racing bikes

For really serious competitors, there are many junior racing bikes on the market. I'll admit – I'm biased when it comes to these types of bikes because I helped design the Mackatak Kids bike by Aquila.

Racing bikes are much lighter and faster than other road or mountain bikes. They have thinner tires, often come with more gears, and are designed with speed in mind, rather than function. This is a bike you're going to train and race on ... not ride to school or take to the corner store.

Here are a few of the features we built into the Mackatak bikes that are worth looking for when buying a first racing bike (for kids under 14):

- A shorter top-tube so you're not too "stretched-out" reaching for the handlebars.
- Shorter cranks (165mm) promote proper spinning technique, and to prevent the possibility of injury.
- We use a "compact-geometry" design so that as the seat height is raised, the effective top-tube length becomes longer, meaning the bike will last longer. The other advantage of this type of geometry is that the sloping top tube allows for excellent stand over clearance – providing added safety.
- Pedals with "Rat Traps" – an excellent way for children to learn to pedal properly and safely! (We'll talk more about that later in this chapter.) Children 14-and-under are not allowed to use clip on style pedals in racing events in Canada, which means that "Rat Trap" style pedals are the best way to develop good pedaling technique until such time as you can use clip-on pedals.
- Solid components. For the Mackatak bike, we chose Shimano's Sora Gruppo, which is solid and dependable. In the end, this brings the price of the bike up, but because we chose to provide an upgraded component package, the bikes tend to last a bit longer, and have a much better resale value.

As you get older and bigger, you'll likely be able to fit on a smaller adult bicycle. While you will be able to use aero bars once you reach the age of 14, it probably doesn't make sense to get a triathlon style frame at this point because, if you are serious about racing, you will likely be getting into draft style racing once you reach the age of 16.

OK, what's a "triathlon style frame" you're asking? Triathlon bikes are designed for riding with aero bars. They typically have a steeper seat tube angle (so you are sitting further forward on the bike) which reduces the stress on your back and hip flexors while riding in the aero position.

In draft-legal racing, you don't actually spend that much time on the aero bars, which can't extend past your brake levers. The bottom line is this: until you're older, you'll be best to stick with a road frame. You'll have many more options available to you, usually at a lesser cost.

Pedals and shoes

Once you are able to use clip-on pedals, they will be a great investment. It isn't until you can really clip on to the pedal that you will be able to truly pedal properly. Proper pedaling involves having your legs work in a circle through the pedal stroke.

Unfortunately, the equipment purchases don't stop there. In order to be able to clip onto the pedals, you will also have to get yourself some cycling shoes. These hard soled shoes have cleats screwed into them, which then clip into the pedals.

There are many different companies that make clip-on pedals and shoes. The most common you'll see are those made by Look and Shimano. Your first set of clip on pedals will likely come when you're buying a bike, which will usually come with one of these style pedals. When you're doing your shopping for a new bike at this stage, remember to keep some money aside to pay for the pedals and/or shoes.

Clothing

Cycling shorts typically have a "chamois" sewn into the seat which provides a bit of padding, making sitting on a hard, thin bicycle seat a little more comfortable. Shirts should be fairly snug fitting so that you don't have too much material flapping in the wind!

Some cyclists like to use cycling gloves while they're out training, but I've never been a fan of using them – my feeling is that since you're not likely to use them racing (it would take too long to pull them on in transition), it doesn't make sense to use them while you're training.

I do strongly suggest using sunglasses while you're out on the bike, though. There's nothing worse than having something fly into your eye while you're riding!

Skill Development

It's important that you are able to handle your bike well. While getting out and riding is a huge step in the right direction, there are also some great drills you can do to help your bike handling skills.

These skills become even more important once you turn 15, and want to participate in draft-legal events. In that style of racing, it's critical that you have mastered many of these skills. These aren't drills you do at 12 and never do again – they should be part of your training regardless of your age!

Braking drills

When using your brakes, it's important to remember to use both your front and rear brakes evenly. If you use only your front brake, you'll fly over the front of the handlebars!

To avoid that happening, you can gradually teach yourself to use your brakes properly.

First, practice stopping and then balancing for a second or two before you put your foot down. Then, practice stopping really quickly. Press on both brakes evenly, and as you stop, slide back along the saddle to get as much of your weight on the back of the bike as you can.

Balance drills

Come to a stop and then balance for as long as you can before putting your foot to the ground or starting to ride again.

Steering drills

Use some cones or water bottles to set up a slalom course. As you get more proficient, move the cones closer together.

Another great way to practice this drill is to go to a parking lot, and ride through the lines. Start by going through every second parking spot, then, as your balance and steering skills improve, go around every line.

Advanced balance drills

Try to pick up a water bottle off a chair or table as you ride by. Once you can do that, put the bottle on the ground, and see if you can pick it up.

Pedals

As discussed in the equipment part of this chapter, clip on pedals aren't allowed in racing for children under 14. That doesn't mean they can't use them in training, but an easier step is to use toe-clips (sometimes referred to as "rat-traps"), which will help you learn to pedal properly.

Toe clips are screwed onto the pedals, and have a strap that can be tightened around the shoe. Even with the straps left very loose, getting a foot into or out of the toe clips while the bike is moving is a tricky endeavor!

Without toe-clips, all you can do when pedaling is push down. With toe-clips, you can learn to add another dimension to the pedaling action, pulling up with one foot while the other pushes down.

One-legged drills

Once you have started to use rat-traps, you will be able to do some one-legged drills. These drills are a great way to improve your pedaling technique. You pull one foot out of the rat-trap, and move yourself forward with just one leg.

Start with by alternating each leg for 15 seconds, and gradually try to build up to where you can do 30-45 seconds at a time.

Once you are 14, and can use clip-on pedals, one-legged drills should become a regular part of your training. Once a week you should do these intervals, and do your best to focus on maintaining a smooth pedal stroke. (You will likely find that you can't keep the pedals moving smoothly through the entire pedal stroke when you first start this drill!).

Standing/Climbing

It's important to be able to feel comfortable "standing" on the bike when you are climbing or sprinting. Standing refers to when you come off the saddle, and all your weight is on your legs and arms.

This takes a bit of getting used to for younger athletes, but you need to practice this because it will come in handy for steep climbs. When you are faced with a tough climb,

sometimes the fastest way up the hill is to get out of the saddle. When you do this, it's important to let the bike swing back and forth between your legs. Don't try to hold the bike completely still underneath you. Keep going in a straight line, but pull on the handlebars so that the bike moves to the right and left underneath you as you move up the hill.

Indoor bike training: Windtrainers

If you live in a spot that has colder winters, you will need to do some of your bike training indoors. One way to do this is on a wind trainer ... a stand that holds the back wheel of your bike and has a resistance wheel that pushes up against your rear tire.

Wind trainers can provide an excellent workout, and can even be useful as a training tool in the summer. They are a great way to do a workout in a short period of time, or can be set up next to a track for a great transition workout. There's a list of indoor workouts that can be done on a wind trainer later in this chapter, and you can learn more about wind trainer transition workouts in the chapter on transition workouts.

Note for parents:

What to look for in a bike program

Many associations (in Canada, the Provincial Governing Bodies, or PGBs, and USAT in the United States) have organized clinics for teenagers to learn the specific biking skills required for riding in a pack. These will often be mandatory for athletes who intend to compete in draft-legal events.

There are two other good resources for getting some help with your child's cycling: the local cycling club, and a local bike shop. Both will often have groups that head out for regular training rides. Make sure that there are either some younger riders heading out in the group, or a designated coach or adult to stay with the kids during the rides.

Many of these groups will have some experienced cyclists who are happy to share their knowledge with young athletes who are eager for experience.

Outdoor workouts

Distance:

30-75 minutes easy paced ride. (Experienced 15- to 16-year-olds can have these rides build to up to 2 hours or more.)

Strength:

1-6 x ~ 400 m hill. Alternate sitting in an easy gear, and standing in a harder gear.

1-4 x ~800m hill. Alternate sitting and standing for parts of each hill.

VO₂ Max:

2-4 x 3 minutes hard/ 2MRI (minute rest interval) of easy spinning

3-5 x 5 minutes hard/ 3MRI

2-3 x 8 minutes hard/ 4MRI

AT:

6-12 x 1 minute hard/ 30SRI

4-8 x 2 minutes hard/ 30SRI

Sprint Training:

4-10 x 1 minute hard/ 2MRI

6-10 x 30 seconds hard/ 1:30RI

Indoor workouts

Technique drill:

30 seconds left leg; 30 seconds right leg; 1 min spin fast – repeat 5 x

Distance:

Commercial/song fartlek: ride the wind trainer in front of the TV, go hard every commercial. You can do the same thing listening to the radio. Song fartleks are the same idea – go hard on certain songs, easier on others. Have fun with these sets!

Lungbuster set: a 15-30 minute ride where you increase the resistance or RPMs every five minutes. Your last 10 minutes should be quite hard. After you're done, take a 5-10 minute warm down

VO$_2$ Max:

20 min drill: 1 x 3 min hard/ 1MRI; 1 x 4min hard/ 2MRI – keep heart rate (HR) higher than you ended three minute interval with; 1 x 5 min hard/ 1MRI – keep HR higher than you ended four minute interval with; 1 x 4 min hard – keep HR higher than you ended 5 min interval with.

AT:

1:30 drill: 15 sec hard/ 1:15RI; 30 sec hard/ 1MRI; 45 sec hard/ 45SRI; 1 min hard/ 30SRI; 1:15 hard/ 15SRI; 1:15 hard/ 15SRI; 1 min hard/ 30SRI; 45 sec hard/ 45SRI; 30 sec hard/ 1MRI; 15 secs hard/ 1MRI

2 minute drill: By 15 sec: 1:45 hard/ 15SRI; 1:30 hard/ 30SRI; 1:15 hard/ 45SRI; 1 min hard/ 1MRI; 1:15 hard/ 45SRI; 1:30 hard/ 30SRI; 1:45 hard/ 15SRI; 2 min hard

20 min crunch set: 4 x 1 min hard/ 15 SRI; 4 min I.B. (increase resistance every 1:20)/ 1MRI; 4 x 1 min hard/ 15SRI; 5 min I.B. (increase resistance every 1:40)

10 min spin drill: 5 min increasing cadence every minute (ideally start at about 75RPM and build to 100RPM); 1 min easy; 3 x 1 min at 90RPM/ 20SRI – try to use one harder gear each time.

CHAPTER 8

Running

Equipment

What to start with

By the time you're 12, if the children in my house are any sort of an example, you're getting some good sized feet! My 12-year-old daughter is a half-size away from being able to wear her mom's shoes. My 10-year-old son has been wearing women's sized running shoes for more than a year, and isn't far away from stealing mom's shoes, either.

Which means a couple of things: you can now get some pretty high-tech running shoes that will help you stay injury-free when training and racing, you have some great choices available so you can find a shoe that is comfortable and fits well, and your training habit is getting expensive!

So, what should you look for in a running shoe? Look for a well-cushioned shoe, with plenty of support that is comfortable.

Just about every shoe company offers a model that fits that description, so picking one out can be difficult. The best thing to do is to speak with a salesperson from a reputable store. They will be able to guide you in the right direction. The salesperson should do a few things before they have you try on a shoe. If they don't do these, run away!

- Ask you what type of running you will be doing, and how often.
- Have a look at your old shoes to see what kind of wear you have put on them. Is the heel worn out? Has the inside of the shoe collapsed? These are tell-tale signs of what sort of a runner you are, and will make a big difference in the type of shoe you will need.
- Ask if you have had any problems with injury. Growing pre-teens and teenagers can have problems with their knees (patella-femoral syndrome), their feet (plantar fasciitis) or their lower legs (shin splints or Achilles tendonitis), problems which require very different types of footwear. Patella-femoral and many lower leg issues require a more supportive shoe, while plantar fasciitis problems and many Achilles tendon problems can be alleviated somewhat with a more flexible shoe.
- Watch you walk and run. Do you pronate or supinate? (Refers to the motion of the foot inwards or outwards as it strikes the ground.) Are you heavy? Light? A heel-striker?

An expert salesperson will evaluate all these factors, and help you pick out the right shoe.

What makes a "running" shoe good for running?

Shoes designed for running will be more flexible than, say, a basketball or a tennis shoe. That "flex" in the shoe allows the foot to roll after the heel hits the ground before the "take-off" point from the toes.

Running shoes won't have the same lateral, or side-to-side, stiffness that you'll find in a tennis or basketball shoe because, for the most part, the running motion doesn't require that kind of protection. The shoes can be a little lighter and provide more protection where it's needed.

How long will a pair of shoes last?

Most running shoes today have amazing soles. The rubber compounds used on the bottom of shoes are incredibly durable. For the most part, what wears out in a pair of shoes is the "mid-sole" – the material between the sole and the upper that provides all the cushioning in the shoe. After repeated pounding, that mid-sole typically "flattens-out" and the show won't provide as much cushioning as it once did.

When you run on a shoe that has lost its mid-sole cushioning, you'll start to feel it. Your knees will ache, you might find you're starting to run into problems with plantar fasciitis, and often people will complain of pain in their lower back because the increased shock of each landing is radiating up their leg.

With adults, the mid-sole of a shoe is typically good for about three to six months, depending on how much running you do. Younger children, typically, won't be affected by the wearing out of the mid-sole of a shoe – they simply outgrow them!

Teenagers can definitely wear out a pair of shoes before they have outgrown them. If that's the case, you'll need to bite the bullet and get another pair. (I'm not sure who I'm addressing that one to – a crying parent or an allowance-poor teen!) Use the old pair of running shoes as "walking-around" shoes until they either outgrow them, or manage to really wear them out!

Racing shoes

Here's a brief look at some of the options available when it comes to racing.

Racing flats are super light shoes designed for speed. To get that way, though, some support and cushioning needs to be sacrificed. For short races, the ones I'm encouraging 12- to 16-year-olds to compete in, they can make a big difference.

Getting the shoe-buying lingo

Here are some of the terms you'll be bombarded with when you walk into the store to buy a pair of running shoes. Memorize these, and you'll be ready to take on any shoe selling pro.

EVA: Ethylene Vinyl Acetate. This is the material you'll find most often in the mid-sole of most running shoes. It's a lightweight and durable material that provides cushioning.

Upper: The fabric part of the shoe that fits over the top of the foot with the laces.

Outsole: The rubber section of the shoe that comes into contact with the ground. Rubber technology has come so far over the last few decades that this is rarely the limiting factor of the life of a shoe. You will flatten out the mid-sole long before you wear out the outsole.

Mid-sole: The layer of material, most often EVA, between the upper and the outsole of the shoe. Manufacturers will often embed other materials (gel pads, air pockets, etc.) to enhance the cushioning provided by the EVA.

Pronation: Too much of an inward roll during the gait cycle.

Supination: Too much of an outward roll during the gait cycle.

Neutral: A running gait that doesn't roll inwards (pronate) or outwards (supinate). It is natural to hate people whose feet fall into this category as they can wear virtually any shoe, or even run bare foot, and never get hurt!

Slip lasted versus board lasted: In order to ensure that light weight trainers stay both light and fast, they will typically be slip-lasted as opposed to board-lasted. Instead of gluing the upper to a board and then attaching the mid-sole (hence the term board lasted!), the upper of racing flats and light-weight trainers are wrapped and stitched down the middle before being glued to the mid-sole.

As with training shoes, it's important to talk to a knowledgeable shoe salesperson or your coach before you buy a pair of racing flats — you might be better off with a lightweight training shoe.

Spikes

An ideal triathlon program will include some track and field training and racing. To compete in track events, you need a pair of spikes.

Spikes are very light shoes with "spikes" underneath the toes and arch of the foot to provide more grip and traction when running on a track.

You have to be careful, though, when you start training in these super-fast shoes. There is next-to-no support, and running hard in them can be a painful experience. Make sure you start wearing them for parts of a few workouts before you race in them. I like to have my athletes start by wearing them for a few intervals within a workout, and then gradually increase the amount of time they're spending in them.

Other clothing choices

Comfortable shorts, singlets and t-shirts that wick moisture away will help appreciably in the summer. A hat with a peak will keep the sun off your face, too.

In the winter, it's important to have some warm tights and a jacket that "breathe" so you don't overheat when you're training.

There are lots of choices available when it comes to clothing, and deciding what you're most comfortable with will be a very personal choice.

Skill development and running drills

When we walk, we're basically leaning forward enough that we're about to fall over, then we catch ourselves, then we lean forward enough that we're about to fall over, then we catch ourselves ... you get the picture.

Running is exactly the same, but we add a bit more momentum to the equation because we add to the "falling over" motion by pushing ourselves forward at the same time.

Here are some things you can work on to improve your running technique:

Arm position

The arms should be bent at 90 degrees at the elbow. The hands should be lightly cupped – never clenched in a fist or held straight out. (Try holding your fingers straight out – you'll see how many tendons and muscles are working hard. That sends lots of blood to those working muscles ... oxygen-filled blood that could be going to the legs!) A great way to practice that optimal hand position is to carry a couple of small sticks during a run.

When swinging your arms, think of swinging them straight back behind you, with the hands coming close to your hips. One of my favorite "image-tools" to describe this process is to suggest that every time your arm swings, you're pulling some money out of your pocket.

"By the end of the run, you'll be rich!" (I know, the kids I coach don't believe me, either.)

Forward lean

The hips should be in front of the foot driving off the ground. The shoulders should be in front of the hips. The whole body should be leaning slightly forward.

Head position

The head should be relaxed; in a position where as few of the neck muscles are working as possible. Look about 20 meters ahead, and scan with your eyes back to the ground directly in front of you. This way you'll be less likely to drop your head to look directly at the ground in front of you.

Drills

An important part of any running program is skill development. Unfortunately, most programs don't spend much time on this all-too-important component of running performance. Even programs that encourage athletes to do some drills during the warm up and warm down fail miserably because there is no attention given to the way those drills are being done.

Take the time to do these drills properly to ensure that you will get the most benefit from them.

Skipping

The first "drill" I ever use with the athletes I work with, regardless of their age (I do this with four-year-olds, I do this with adults!), is skipping.

The first step is to skip for about 10- or 15-meters, swinging your arms naturally.

Next you continue to skip, but this time try "going for height." Now you're trying to push off the foot to get as much air-time as possible. As you push off, drive the opposite knee up to help get more height.

Once you've done two to four repetitions of skipping for height, the next step is to "go for distance." Now the emphasis goes from pushing straight up off the back foot to pushing along the ground with that back foot. When done correctly, you should feel the muscles in your upper thigh working.

Mach drills

After a few weeks of working on the skipping drill, the next step in the drill progression is what we call "Mach" drills.

Developed by Canadian sprinting coach Gerard Mach, these drills isolate each part or phase of the running motion, enabling you to develop both skill and strength in each phase of your stride.

Each drill should be done walking at first, and then you can do them with a skip between each stride.

The "A" drill

The emphasis with the "A" drill is to fully extend the driving leg. As the left leg pushes off the ground, the right leg bends at both the hip and the knee, creating 90 degree angles at both. The right foot is brought straight back to the ground, and then becomes the driving leg while the left leg bends up.

Most people, when doing the "A" drill, will try to bring their knee up too high – the knee only has to get high enough so the upper leg is parallel to the ground.

The "B" drill

The next progression after the "A" drill works on the "pulling-back" motion of the leg into the ground. This is a critical phase in the running stride – the quicker the leg can get back to the ground the faster the runner's turnover will be. When this is coupled with efficient positioning of the hips (ahead of the drive foot), you will not only increase your turnover, you will also increase your stride length because all of your energy will go into moving you forward.

The "B" drill starts in the same way as the "A" drill, but instead of bringing the foot straight back to the ground, you now extend the flexed leg forward, and pull the foot quickly back to the ground.

The "C" drill

This is the easiest of the three Mach drills to master. The "C" drill is simply a "bum-kick!"

This drill is designed to emphasize the recovery phase of the leg, when it bends back and then moves forward. Lift your leg up behind you, kicking yourself in the behind as you go.

It's important to remember to swing your arms correctly (remember, pull that cash out of your pockets!) and quickly as you do this drill. Emphasizing turnover is an essential coaching tool during the "C" drill – I always try to emphasize to think of having "quick feet."

Run training

How far is too far?

As a race announcer, I am often inspired by some of the impressive performances I see at many events. I am

not inspired, though, when I see young athletes running much further than they should.

These days it's not uncommon for 10-year-olds to compete in 10km events. Lately I have been amazed at the number of 18-year-olds who compete at Ironman distances. Those distances are far too long at that age! Sure, these kids and teenagers are capable of completing the distance, but doing so only jeopardizes any future they might have in the sport.

Not only are pre-teens and young teenagers who run much too far considerably more likely to get injured or "burned out," but running too far, too young, can prevent a very talented athlete from reaching his or her true potential.

To compete at the highest levels in any sport, an athlete must have a certain level of "bottom-end" speed. This refers to their ability to run fast. Once you lose your natural speed, it is almost impossible to get it back. Running long distances at a young age tends to affect the ability to run faster once you get older.

The kids who complete those long distances at a young age are often the ones who end up being the "pacers" in races – they are the ones who are at the front for most of the race, only to get passed in the closing stages by someone with a faster kick.

"Who cares," you might be saying. "I'm not going to be a world class athlete. I just want to have fun."

All I can say to that is this: what you're thinking as a 12-year-old might change dramatically if you suddenly become a successful 15-year-old triathlete. If you've lost all your bottom-end speed, though, you're never going to reach the potential you might have.

Competing with the best in the world requires much more than just talent. It requires a drive and determination ... and patience! The only thing that you are likely to do by running too much, too soon, is to guarantee that you won't become the athlete you could have.

Training

Once you're 12 or older, an ideal triathlon program includes work with a track group. It's important to get running guidance from a coach who can pay attention to the details required for top-notch running training. It's important to develop good technique and endurance to be a successful triathlete, but first and foremost at this stage in your development is getting fast!

Too many young triathletes quickly get drawn to running longer events. I see so many athletes from various triathlon programs competing in 5km races on a regular basis, rather than taking part in a track event that would be a much better way to develop their triathlon potential.

Need proof?

At the very first Olympic men's triathlon event, held in Sydney, Australia in 2000, Canada's Simon Whitfield and Germany's Stefan Vukovic were running side by side with one kilometer to go in the race. Their competition was well behind them, so they knew that the race would come down to a sprint for the line.

Afraid that he wouldn't be able to beat Whitfield, who had been a track and field runner in high school, Vukovic tried to pull away. Whitfield was able to stay with the German, and as the finish line came in sight, sprinted away to the Olympic Gold medal. How sure was Vukovic that he couldn't keep up? He slowed to almost a walk, and started celebrating with the crowd! He knew that he didn't have the kind of speed he needed to win, so he decided to enjoy the silver medal he was assured of.

If your dream is to someday be competitive with the best in the world, remember that you need to be fast. It doesn't matter how far you can go as a 12-year-old, although it is important that you do some training to be able to cover your race distance. Even if you're not the fastest sprinter or middle-distance runner at your school, it's important that you work on some shorter events. I like to see 12- to 16-year-olds compete in as many 400, 800 and 1,500m events as possible.

I know it is fun to win, and sometimes you might feel like you could be winning the local 5km road race rather than coming third or fourth in an 800m race on the track. Remember, though, that the track race is likely to help you compete better as a triathlete, and might help you win a triathlon event some day!

What to look for in a coach or track program

While you want to find a coach or program that will help you develop your running speed and technique, you need to find a coach and a program that won't be so demanding of your time and energy that you won't be able to pursue your swimming and biking if your goal is to compete as a triathlete.

Ideally you should find a group that meets two or three times a week for workouts, and has a flexible race schedule that will allow you to compete in as many races as you'd like, but not so many that you won't have time for any other events through the year!

Fartlek training

So you're at the park, hooking up with the local running club for the first time. You've been an avid triathlete now for a while, and you've decided that it's time to improve your running. Mom or Dad dropped you off at the park to meet with the group. So far, so good.

Then the coach tells you that the workout for the night is a fartlek session through the trails. "Fartlek?" you think to yourself. "What on earth is a fartlek?"

No, the coach isn't trying to make fun of you because you're a triathlete, or because you might have some gas. Fartlek is a Swedish word that means, literally, speed play. Fartlek training involves run workouts where there is a wide variety of speeds and efforts. It is a fun way to add intervals to your training program.

You don't have to be an elite runner to get benefits from adding fartlek workouts to your run training regimen. It is a great way to work on your speed and strength while also providing variety to your program.

Fartlek workouts can be totally unstructured, where the distance and time intervals are randomly picked. These workouts can also be completely structured, where each interval has a set distance or time, and a set recovery period.

Advanced runners can make a fartlek session one of the hardest workouts in their repertoire, especially when done in a group. Always eager to push their training partners to the limit, each runner will try to outdo the next by picking harder and harder intervals.

A Shot On Site

Some workouts

With a group

Free Fartlek

Take turns deciding the next interval. The leader for each interval controls the pace, and the distance of that interval. Rotate around the group so each runner has a chance to do lead a couple of workouts.

Blind Fartlek

Everyone in the group is given a number, but everyone keeps their number secret. The runners go in order, trying to surprise the rest of the group as they start each interval and forcing the group to react to them.

Workouts alone or with a group

Telephone Pole Fartlek

One pole hard/one pole easy; two hard/two easy; three hard/three easy; then repeat the cycle in reverse. You can repeat this set as many times as you can in, say, 20 minutes. To make the set even harder, shorten the recovery to one light post.

Timed Fartleks

Run hard for a given time, recover for a specific time. For example, go hard for four minutes and then recover for four minutes. To make this set even harder, do the recovery pace at a steady training pace, ensuring that you never feel completely recovered as you start the next set. You can vary the times for this set depending on what part of the season you're in. Early season you might want to do longer intervals of four to eight minutes. During the season you might want to shorten the interval and lengthen the recovery to work on your speed.

Distance Fartlek

On a specific course, designate different parts as hard, and others as easy. You can make this as short as a loop around the park, or as long as an 8 mile run.

Five-minute drill

This is a great fartlek workout you can do on a track. More advanced and elite competitors will try to finish a mile during this set. Start with 30 seconds of hard running, followed by 30 seconds of steady running. That's followed by 15 seconds hard, with 15 seconds recovery. That cycle is repeated twice, then there's one more 30 second hard interval with a 30 second recovery, followed by one last hard interval for one minute.

If you don't have a coach to come up with the workout, use your own imagination to develop some fun fartlek sessions. Remember, it's all about play, with some speed mixed into the translation, too.

Hill training

Fighting gravity is a great way to develop some strength in your running. It's an easy thing to incorporate into your training program. Find yourself a hill, run to it, go up and down it a few times, then run home!

It doesn't have to be that simple ... and boring, though. If you have lots of hills around where you live, try to find some different types of hills to run on. One week you could incorporate a longer, more gradual hill. The next week you could get your workout done on a shorter, steeper hill. Some of my favorite hill workouts incorporate a bit of both – I try to find a spot where I have access to a short, steep hill and a long, gradual one, and alternate between the two.

Don't do too many hills in a session, though. Build up gradually through your early season of training, maybe adding one hill each week. Rather than doing more than, say, eight hills in a session, you might want to add a bit of running off the top of the hill – anywhere from 50-100m. This is a great way to get yourself into the habit of working hard not only up the hill, but after you've gone over the top.

The top of the hill is a spot where many people want to slow down and recover, which gives you a great chance to open a gap on them!

In terms of technique, it's very important to remember to lean forward as you're going up a hill, and to take shorter steps. This will conserve energy, and also put you in just the right position to maximize your speed as you climb.

Stair training

A great way to develop some leg power is to do some training on stairs.

Where we live in Hamilton, we have a number of sets of stairs that go up the escarpment that separates the two parts of the city. There are 500 stairs in one of those sets, but I don't make my athletes train on those too often!

We break our stair workouts into a few different phases. After a warm up, we do some drills on the stairs. We do the "A" drill mentioned earlier up a flight or two, followed by a run down those same stairs to recover. Then we might do three or four flights of stairs, taking them two at a time. We'll follow that up with the same number, but this time taking them one at a time. Then we'll alternate doing five stairs hopping on one leg, followed by five stairs on the other ... a set we'll repeat two or three times. We follow that up with another three or four flights taken two at a time ... then repeat the whole process again!

Interval workouts

If you think of fartlek training as speed play, interval workouts are a more formal approach to doing a hard run session. Interval workouts don't have to take place on a track. You can do interval workouts on a grass field, a road loop, or along a measured stretch of trail.

Interval workouts have a defined distance, and a defined rest "interval." They are most often associated with a track, which is where I'll start.

Setting up an interval workout on the track can be a lot of fun. The options are endless, so don't limit yourself to my suggestions – see how imaginative you can be with your own workouts. You can also try to combine some of the different sets.

VO$_2$ Max:

2-4 x 800 m/ 3MRI (minutes rest interval)

1-2 x 1000 m/ 4MRI

AT:

4-8 x 200 m/ 30SRI (seconds rest interval)

4-8 x 200 m/ 200 m brisk jog recovery

2-6 x 400 m/ 30SRI

Sprint Training:

3-6 x 200 m/ 200 m walk recovery

4-8 x 400 m/ 2:30 RI (rest interval)

CHAPTER 9

Transition Workouts

Sometimes known as "Brick" workouts, transition workouts are a fun way to practice the transition from bike to run – one of the hardest parts of any triathlon race.

There are a couple of different ways to practice this – you can do a one longer bike followed by a run, or you can do a number of shorter bike-to-run sets.

As youngsters, my children used to watch their mom and dad do sets of 2.5km of biking followed by a 400m run loop that we could do right from our house. The kids came up with their own version of a transition workout – bike to one stop sign at the end of the street, ride back, and then run to the stop sign at the other end of the street and run back.

By the time you're 12 you are ready to take make these transition workouts more structured, and a more integral part of your regular training routine. These transition sets will help you develop an ability to run hard off the bike. They will help you become faster at what has become a critical part of junior racing ... either getting your shoes and helmet on before grabbing your bike and running out of transition, or racking your bike and taking off your helmet before you start the run.

The ideal situation for this type of workout is a road loop that is closed to traffic. While we don't have quite that idyllic a set up where I live in Hamilton, we do have a 750m loop that doesn't have much traffic. This provides many different options: we can do a 750m bike followed by a short run (we cone off a 300m run loop on the grass on the inside of the loop), or do two loops of the oval for a 1.5km ride, followed by a 750m run. This set can be repeated a number of times, depending on the age of the athlete.

Another great way to do a transition workout is to take a windtrainer to a track. You can do a timed interval on the windtrainer, followed by a 400m lap of the track. This is another set that can be repeated a number of times.

Race simulation transition workouts

You won't have a good idea how fast you can go in a race unless you have done some workouts over your race distance. Race simulation sets are designed to allow you work at your goal race pace, so that when you're in the event, there won't be any surprises!

These workouts should start at half your race distance, and eventually build to about 2/3 to 3/4 of your race distance.

Here are some transition workouts you can try yourself:
(Note: All of these workouts should start with a 10 minute warm-up on the bike and a five minute warm-up for the run. There should be a warm-down of about five minutes on both the bike and the run, followed by some gentle stretching.)

Distance oriented:

- 3-10 x {1.5km bike/ 400m run}
- 6-15 x {750m bike/ 250m run}
- 2-6 x {3km bike/ 750m run}

Windtrainer/Track sets:

- 4-10 x {3 minutes hard/ 400m run}
- 2-6 x {5 minutes hard/ 800m run}

Race simulation sets:

- 1-2 x {10km bike/ 2km run} 5 MRI between sets
- 1-2 x {12km bike/ 3km run} 10 MRI between sets

In the summer, if you have access to a pool, you can add a swim to the workout the simulation set. A 200-meter swim followed by a bike and a run that's about 2/3 of your race distance is a great way to practice the swim-to-bike transition.

During these sets, do your best to follow all of the rules you will have to follow in a race. Run out of the "transition area" with your bike to a designated "mount-dismount" line. Ensure that you put your helmets on properly, and in Canada, make sure to put the helmet on before grabbing your bike. (See "Transition area set up" on p. 111.)

Equipment for transition workouts

It's great if you have the ability to set up some bike racks so you can practice "racking" your bike the same way you will in a race, but it isn't a necessity in order to have a successful transition workout.

If you are old enough to be allowed to race with cycling shoes, make sure you practice getting into and out of your cycling and running shoes during your transition sets. One way to make sure your cycling shoes stay in the right position as you come out of the transition area is to use a rubber band to hold them in place. Once your foot is in the pedal, and you're ready to go, all you have to do is start pedaling and the band will snap!

No matter how old you are, getting some elastic laces for your running shoes will make a big difference for your transition workouts and during your races. These laces don't need to be tied – they will simply slip onto your feet, ensuring a speedy trip through the transition area!

A winter version of a transition set can be done at a gym using stationary bikes and rowing machines or stair climbers for the bike.

CHAPTER 10

Strength Training

While recent research has shown that weight training for young adults isn't as harmful as once thought, to this day I remain hesitant to have young athletes do much in the weight room. I am much happier to have them use their own body weight for strength workouts.

Strength training is an important component to any training program. With the young athletes I've worked with, gains in strength have lead to improvements in their performances. I like to utilize as much circuit training as possible when it comes to strength training, no matter what the age. There are times, though, when incorporating some weights into the program can help, which is why I have included some weight training suggestions in this section.

The most important goal from a strength program is to try and prevent any muscle imbalances that might develop from swimming, biking or running. Muscle imbalances happen when one group of muscles gets really strong, while the opposite set of muscles in the body don't develop to the same extent. As a young tennis player, I became so much stronger on my right side that at one point the muscles on the right side of my back were four times as developed as those on the left.

A more common problem for growing pre-teens and teenagers are knee problems that develop from an over-development of either the quadriceps (the four muscles on the front of your thigh) or your hamstrings (the muscles behind your leg). Making sure that you do exercises to ensure that neither muscle group becomes too strong can alleviate some of the problems.

Some important notes to remember when it comes to weight training for 12- to 16-year-olds (many of these notes hold true for adults, too!):
- As with any hard workout, make sure to give yourself a full 48 hours to recover between weight workouts. (Yes, you will find many programs that suggest that doing an upper body strength session one day followed by a lower body session the next day. I, personally, don't like that idea for a few reasons: your body doesn't truly have time to recover between hard sessions, and it also has you doing strength workouts far more often than you likely should as a triathlete.)
- Use of very heavy weight should be avoided.
- Strength sessions shouldn't take much longer than 15 to 20 minutes. These workouts should be augmenting swim, bike and run training ... not become workouts in-and-of themselves.

Before we talk about weight training, though, let me tell you about my favorite type of strength training.

Circuit training

The hallowed halls of Rugby school in England – the place where C. Webb Ellis "first picked up the ball and ran" way back in 1824 – gave me my first introduction to the world of circuit training. It was there, every afternoon, immediately after classes and before rugby practice began, that the school's fitness addicts would congregate at the gym for a half-hour circuit session.

This was no circuit for the meek: the goal of the school's physical education teachers, as far as I could tell, was to push those silly enough to try this workout into a state of complete exhaustion.

To finish two rounds of Rugby's famous circuit was a feat that few athletes managed.

What could be so hard, you ask? The exact details of the workout have long passed through my memory (the body doesn't care to remember too many painful things), but I remember minute long intervals of push ups, sit ups, dips, rope climbs, box jumps, chin ups, wind sprints, and balance beam walks. Balance beam walks, you ask? This was so tough, you wonder? All I remember is the fear I felt as I climbed to the beam, which was placed a good 10 feet in the air, and wondering if my exhausted legs and arms would be able to break the fall I was sure I would make.

I never did, and my three-month stint at England's famous school introduced me to many things. The most enduring, though, has been circuit training.

What makes this form of training so good is that it can be done anywhere, and offers the most time efficient way to get a workout done.

Fitness trails you see in many parks are great examples of a basic circuit. Stations are set up, and you simply run from one to the other doing things like chin ups, push ups, jumps, and abdominal curls, separated by a short run.

By combining strength and cardiovascular exercises together with a very short recovery (if you really want to show off your stuff, you can skip the recovery completely), you get a muscle and stamina workout all at once. To get the cardiovascular benefits, you need to work hard and feel your heart beating quickly throughout the entire set – and that isn't always easy.

Not everyone has access to gyms like the one I worked in at Rugby, but that shouldn't stop you. The only limiting factor for setting up a circuit is your imagination. I've had athletes do them on the side of a pool, or even in a school hall. Some of my best circuits have taken place in hotel rooms, city parks, and my own living room.

Typically, I map out a workout area with different stations in different parts of the room. I might do push ups in one corner, abdominal curls in another, burpees or "Russian splits" in the center of the room, dips using a chair or a couch, go back to my abdominal spot for another set, do another set of push ups for good measure, and finish off the entire circuit by doing "chair squats" until my quads don't like me anymore. (See glossary on p. 95 for a definition of the different exercises.)

I either do my circuit for time or by a certain number of repetitions. Often I will work for 30 seconds, and recover for 10. Other days I will complete 15 reps of each exercise, and see how long it takes to complete the set. Then after a short break, I try to improve my time. The number of sets will depend on how much time I have, and how much my arms and legs will take!

When you do a circuit right, it can be a very tough workout.

At one club I used to work at, I set up a circuit workout three days a week in the aerobics studio. Exercise mats were used for abdominal curls and push ups. I had the athletes do wind sprints along the length of the floor. We had a chin-up bar placed in one corner. We also used skipping ropes, benches for dips, and a flight of stairs which we could run up and down. All told, I set up 15 exercises, and paired off the participants so there was always someone there to keep them honest. By the end of the hour long circuit, all 30 crazy circuit types were completely exhausted.

Which is exactly the way I always felt in that old gym in England. Mr. Ellis might have run with the ball and created a new sport, but I will always remember Rugby school for so much more – my introduction to the best workout I know.

Things to keep in mind:

- Always warm up, and stretch before you start your circuit. The exercises can be very strenuous, and it is critical that your muscles are ready to work hard! The best time to do a circuit is after another workout, when you're warmed up.
- If you have any problems with a specific exercise, simply skip it. Always err on the side of caution – work hard, but don't strain anything!
- Older athletes (15-and-up) should consider adding weights to their circuit: if you have some dumbbells at home, add a set of biceps curls or triceps extensions to the circuit. (See weight training exercises below.)
- Don't do a circuit two days in a row – always give yourself at least one full day to recover. Your muscles actually develop during this time. The workout breaks down the muscle tissue, which puts itself together during your recovery. If you want to do a workout on the off days, do an easy cardiovascular session.

Example Circuits

No equipment:
- Push ups
- Abdominal curls
- Dips
- Burpees
- Push ups
- Abdominal Curls
- Chair squats

Do 30 seconds of each exercise, take 10 seconds recovery. Repeat the set 3-5 times, taking an extra 30 second break between exercises. (Other exercises you can easily add: step ups, stair climbs, chin ups.)

Weight Equipment:
- Leg Press
- Leg Curl
- Leg Extension
- Lat Pull Downs
- Bench Press
- Shoulder Press
- Biceps Curls
- Triceps Extensions

Do 30 seconds or 20 reps of each exercise. Between each, do a hard run or bike for one to two minutes.

Some basic equipment:
- Squats (Chair or with weight)
- Chin ups (hands facing you)
- Step ups
- Dips
- Abdominal curls
- Triceps Extensions
- Bike ride
- Chin ups (hands facing away from you)
- Skipping
- Push ups

- Abdominal curls
- Biceps Curls
- Wind sprints
- Dips

Do 30 seconds of each strength exercise, one to two minutes of each "cardio" exercise. Repeat the set two to three times.

Glossary of some unfamiliar terms

- Dips: Put your hands on a chair at shoulder width. With your legs straight out in front of you, lower your butt to the ground (but don't rest it there!) by bending your arms so they are bent at 90 degrees at the elbow. Push yourself back up.
- Burpees: Start from a standing position, bend down and put your hands on the ground next to your feet. Push your feet straight out behind you so you are in a "push up" position. Bring your feet back under your shoulders, straighten up, and jump in the air. One down, 14 to go!
- Squats (Chair): Start standing straight up in front of a chair. Keeping your back straight, bend your knees as if you were sitting down until your butt is almost touching the chair. Straighten up, again keeping your back straight.
- Russian Splits: With your left foot in front of your right, bend your knees until your hands are touching the ground. Jump up in the air, straightening your back and switching legs as you go. As you come back to the ground, bend your knees until your hands are touching the ground again. One down ...

Weight training

Anyone who has watched an Olympic marathon knows that the best runners are, well, to put it bluntly, not "muscle heads"! The more weight you have to carry around, the harder it is to run fast. While triathletes do need to have a bit more muscle mass for swimming and cycling, you don't want to be too big.

As with the circuit training outlined earlier, preventing muscle imbalances is the first goal of weight training. Performance will only be enhanced with more strength if your technique will make use of the added strength. Until your technique is nearly perfect, the weight training you do isn't going to help you go faster. It will, however, make you less likely to get injured.

Also, as mentioned earlier in this chapter, weight training should be restricted to older athletes – ideally those 15 and older.

So what should your weight program look like? It should be a general strength program covering all the basic muscle groups. Here's an example of a weight program I suggest for junior athletes:

Exercise	Number of repetitions
Leg Extensions/ Leg Curls	15-20
Lat Pull Downs	8-12
Bench Press	8-12
Shoulder Press	8-12
Biceps Curls	8-12
Triceps Extensions	8-12
Abdominal curls	30-50 (split into sets of 10-15)

With this program, I suggest that once you reach the maximum number of repetitions, you raise the weight that you're using to make the exercise more challenging.

Planking

A great way to augment either a circuit or weight training program is to add some "planking." This is an exercise where you support yourself on your elbows and your feet, holding your back as straight as possible.

You should start by holding the position for about 10 seconds, then taking a break. You can repeat the exercise a few times. As you get stronger, you can add some variations to the plank, like lifting one leg up, or lifting one arm up behind your back.

• regular plank

Another excellent exercise is the side plank, where you support yourself on one elbow.

A great planking set would look something like this:

15-60 seconds regular plank/ 30SRI
30-60 seconds side plank – each side
30-60 seconds plank, alternating 5 seconds each of: left leg up, right leg up, left arm behind the back and right arm behind the back.

• arm up

• leg up

• side plank

Stability Ball Training

Like planking, working with a Stability, or "Swedish," ball can be a great way to augment your strength training. We have a number of these balls in our training room in our basement, and our children love to play on them. These balls are a great way to work on what we call "core" strength – which refers to the strength of your abdominal and low back muscles.

Stability balls come in a number of different sizes, so make sure you're using one that fits you properly. A ball that fits will allow you to have your back parallel to the ground when your feet are on the ball, and your arms are straight.

Here are some great exercises you can do on a Stability Ball:

- Knee to the ball
- Legs in and out from a modified plank position
- Hamstring curls

- Balancing on your knees
- Standing on the ball
- Abdominal curls

Medicine Ball

Another favorite activity for young athletes I coach is working with a medicine ball. It's important to make sure you're not using a ball that is too heavy when participating in this activity – I don't like to see kids under 14 using anything heavier than 2kg (4.4 pounds).

Older athletes can use heavier balls, but should do so only if they have got good strength training under their belt, and if they are using good technique.

Some exercises you can do with a medicine ball include:

- Throwing from between the legs – make sure to keep your back straight, and to bend at your knees NOT your waist

- Throwing from the side

- Overhead throws

- Push Throws

- Abdominal curls

CHAPTER 11
Flexibility

Any training program must include stretching. The best time to include stretching in any activity is during the warm-up and warm-down part of a workout.

Flexibility is a critical component to athletic performance. The stiffer the muscles are, the more likely they are to become injured. The more flexible you are, the more performance you will get out of your body.

Here are a few key stretches that you should include in your training routines to enhance their flexibility:

Hamstrings and low back

The "hang-ten" stretch: Stand with the feet shoulder width apart, knees slightly bent, and bend at the waist so the hands either touch the ground, or get as close to it as possible.

Quad stretch

Reach behind the back using the left hand and grab your right foot. Pull straight back to create the stretch in the quadriceps muscles (The ones in the front of the upper leg!). Do the same with the left leg, using the right hand to grab it.

Calf Stretch

Put one foot ahead of the other while leaning against a wall. Straighten the back leg out to stretch the calf muscles (the ones at the back of your lower leg).

Obliques

With feet a little wider than shoulder width apart, support the right hand on the right knee, straighten the left arm up over the head, and lean to the right side.

Shoulders

Reach the right arm across the body so the hand ends up behind the left shoulder. Grab the right elbow with the left hand to help pull (gently!) the arm a bit further. Repeat the process with the left arm.

Groin

Sitting on the ground, put the feet together in front. Grab the ankles with each hand, and use the forearm to push gently down on the legs.

Each stretch should be held for about 10- to 15-seconds. Never "bounce" during the stretch – make it a smooth, sustained motion.

These are just a few basic stretches. Different sports will often require an emphasis on flexibility in specific areas. When you're working with your swim, bike and running coaches, make sure they are taking the time to stretch and warm up for each workout. If your coaches don't, then make sure you add some stretching when you get home from practice!

CHAPTER 12

Nutrition

As a coach, people I work with often ask me about various new "diets" they have heard about and want to try. I always ask them one simple question when they ask me about one of these diets – can you see yourself on this diet for the rest of your life?

As you hit your teenage years, you are going to be bombarded by a number of miracle diets that promise the world. It's important to remember that nutrition is a multi-million dollar industry that has lots of money to advertise, and to influence stories in newspapers, magazines and on television. At a time when you're likely going through some monstrous body changes, the messages you'll see are very tempting. Unfortunately, they're typically very short term solutions to an issue that doesn't have a quick fix.

Proper nutrition, like physical activity, should be part of your lifestyle. It's not something you do for a week or two, then take a few weeks away from.

In Canada, we have an amazing nutritional resource that has been put together by the government offering a reasonable eating guide. It's called "Canada's Food Guide," and it provides appropriate amounts of food from each of the four food groups. A range of serving sizes is provided for each group. Younger children should choose a lower number of servings, while male teenagers would eat the higher number of servings.

The four food groups are:
• Grain Products: 5-12 servings per day. A serving would include one slice of bread, 30 grams of cereal. Two servings would include a cup (250ml) of pasta or rice.
• Vegetables and Fruit: 5-10 servings per day. A serving would include a medium size vegetable or fruit, or a cup of salad.
• Milk Products: Youth 10-16 years, 3-4 servings per day; Adults 2-4 servings per day. A serving includes one cup of milk or two slices (50g) of cheese.
• Meat and Alternatives: 2-3 servings per day. A serving includes 50-100 grams of meat, poultry or fish, or 2 tablespoons (30ml) of peanut butter.

Moderation is the key to every healthy diet. It's OK to have the occasional bag of potato chips or piece of chocolate. It's when these not-so-healthy choices become a regular occurrence that you can begin to get into trouble.

So much of nutrition comes down to common sense. We all have a pretty good idea of what we should and shouldn't be eating ... it's getting ourselves to follow that common sense that isn't always easy!

Fueling for performance

If you're looking for a good sports nutrition resource, you can't go wrong to follow anything Nancy Clarke has written. A practicing registered dietician from Boston, Mass. in the United States, Clarke has a realistic approach to eating for athletes. She is not a huge fan of supplements. She suggests that you are much better to get the vitamins and minerals you need from regular food.

Clarke talks about "fueling" for athletic performance, both in training and racing. She emphasizes the importance of getting the right kind of food into your body at the right time in order to perform.

Intuitively, you already know that. If you skip breakfast and lunch, you know that you're not going to have a good running practice after school. If you want to perform well, you need to make sure that your body has enough energy to do what is asked of it.

Energy drinks, bars and gels

For races and training sessions of less than an hour, your body shouldn't need any extra fuel during the activity. Certainly, on hot days you'll want to have some water, but your body should have enough energy stored to get you through the workout. Research has shown, though, that after the workout, your body will recover more quickly if you get some food into your system within about 30 minutes.

One thing you do want to avoid, though, while you're training and racing, is what we call "bonking." It's also often referred to as "hitting the wall" … a time when you simply run out of energy and are forced to slow down or stop.

As a teenager, you shouldn't really be doing workouts long enough to get you to that point, but you will likely start to do workouts that last longer than an hour, especially on the bike. At this point you might want to take some extra fuel with you. For workouts up to a couple of hours, taking some sort of an electrolyte replacement drink, like

Gatorade, will do the trick. There are a number of types of drinks on the market, and deciding which one to use can be difficult. Find one that you like to drink (tastes good!) and seems to give you enough energy while you're working out. As an athlete, I tended to use Gatorade for training because it was readily available and I enjoyed the various flavors.

PowerBar, the original energy bar, was developed by a Canadian marathon runner named Brian Maxwell, who kept "bonking" during his marathon races. He developed an energy bar could be easily digested while he was running, and the resulting product, PowerBar, has become the industry leader in energy bars.

PowerBars, and the various other products like it, are also a useful energy source during workouts. These can also be a great snack or post-race food. They shouldn't become a main source of your energy ... you're still best to get many of your nutrients from regular food.

There are different types of energy bars available these days – everything from elaborate breakfast bars to protein bars to those designed specifically for training and racing. Hard training teenagers can use these products as healthy snacks and ways to get more calories into their calorie-craving bodies ... but, remember, moderation is important.

Gels have become increasingly popular over the last decade or so, and offer a quick energy source during long distance training and racing. Once again, young athletes shouldn't be racing and competing in events much longer than 90 minutes, which means these products shouldn't be necessary during racing, but they can be a good energy source during longer training sessions.

Note to Parents:

The lifestyle component of nutrition is even more important for your children if they are participating in a serious training program. It's critical that we start them off right. The eating habits you help your children develop in their early years have a huge impact on the rest of their lives.

Childhood obesity is a huge problem with young children these days. Much of that can be attributed to poor eating habits. We all know intuitively that we shouldn't be eating foods laden with fat and sugar, yet we often make those kinds of food choices because those types of foods are so readily available. In the busy, go-go-go lifestyle many of us lead, we often make our choices based on convenience rather than our health.

We can't afford to make those kinds of choices with our children, though ... especially if we want to enhance their active, sporting, lifestyles!

Starting the day off right with a good breakfast is critical, especially with busy, active children in the house. In the Mackinnon household, we have a simple breakfast rule that gets the day off to a good nutritional start – breakfast needs to include something from at least three different food groups. From there on in, it's much easier to complete the day's quota from each of the food groups.

As in physical activity, role modeling when it comes to eating is really important. Kids don't miss a thing – and if they see you making poor food choices, they're likely going to follow suit!

CHAPTER 13

Race Preparation

The Psychology of training and racing

While virtually every topic in this manual warrants an entire book, there is none that deserves more attention than this one. I will be brief here not because this isn't an important part of your triathlon preparation, but rather because you are best to follow up with some other resources.

Too often we get caught up in the final result of our races, and forget about the most important part of the competition – the actual process of swimming, biking and running. The way to get yourself to the finish line the fastest is to do well in those three disciplines. Worrying about who you may or may not beat along the way won't help you do that.

As you race, think about your technique. This will help you focus on the things that will make you go faster. Don't just say to yourself, "Bike faster!" Go through the different techniques that will help you do that. Are you pedaling properly, could you be more aerodynamic?

Try to be nice to yourself. Too many hard-hearted athletes say the nastiest things to themselves while they are on a race course. Deciding you're a worthless athlete half way through an event won't help anyone. Would you say that to a friend? Be positive. Positive race results will follow.

Just three tips, but believe me, they aren't easy to utilize in the heat of competition. You need to practice them during your training. Just like all the other components, your mental fitness must never be neglected.

Peaking

Peaking is the term used to describe your training as you go into a race. I always say, if you are going to race, make sure you're ready to really race. Otherwise, stay at home and do a workout.

Now that doesn't mean that you are going to be in your best racing shape for every race of the year. What it means is that for every race you should give your body some rest so it can perform properly in the race situation.

For relatively unimportant races, simply backing things off a couple of days before will be quite enough of a peak. I suggest to the athletes I coach that they take a day off two days before the race. The day before the race is used to get some "sharpness" into the arms and legs in preparation for the next day's race. Short workouts with some "pick-ups" – short sprints to loosen things up – will help you prepare.

As you get closer to your major race or races of the year, rest becomes more important than any other part of your training. By the time you get to the last three weeks of your training, you are pretty much as fit as you are going to get. All you can do from that point on is maintain your fitness and work on your speed going into the big day. Do some sessions that will simulate the race, e.g. a transition workout at roughly the same time and over the same terrain as the event. Practice those psychological exercises. Most of all, relax. Look back at all the workouts you have behind you to reassure yourself that you are fit and ready to race.

Race day

The day is finally here. You've been training for months, and now it's time to get ready for the race. Here are a few tips that will make the day a bit easier:

- Eat something about 90 minutes before the race. Your breakfast should be easily digested foods that you have tried eating before workouts with success. My personal favorite is a banana, bottle of Gatorade, and either a piece of toast or a PowerBar.
- Get to the race site early. There's nothing worse than being nervous ... and finding yourself rushing around to get everything together.
- Pack your bag carefully – the day before the race! Make a list of everything you will need, and check off the items as you put them in your bag

- Set up your transition area. Put a towel down next to your bike, and put your running shoes at the back of the towel (if you are old enough to use cycling shoes in the race), or at the front of the towel if you're going to be using them on the bike. Put your helmet next to those, with sunglasses inside if you intend to wear them during the race. You should attach your race number to a race belt, which should be next to your helmet. Rehearse your transition strategy a few times in the morning.
- Walk from the swim exit to your bike a few times to make sure you know exactly where to go.
- Follow a warm-up plan that you have practiced a few times during transition workouts. I like to do a short bike ride, followed by a short run with some strides about 45 minutes before the race. Then, with about 15 minutes to go, if the water is warm enough, I do a short swim warm-up before heading off to the start.
- Have fun!

Race strategy

It's important to have some ideas of how you're going to approach the race before you start. I try to have a chat with the athletes I coach before their races so I can go through some ideas with them about what they should be thinking about during the race.

If you have a coach, try to come up with a race plan a few days before the race. Here are some of the things I like to include in the race plan:

- Start: I suggest picking a side of the start line suited to your swimming talents. If you are a strong swimmer, then it makes sense to stay near the middle of the start area, where you're more likely to find some fast swimmers to draft behind. (Drafting, where you stay right behind another athlete and are able to go faster because they are breaking the wind or helping you move faster through the water, isn't allowed in most races on the bike, but is allowed during the swim. You can go quite a bit faster if you can stay on someone's feet during the swim portion of the race.) If you're a weaker swimmer, stick to one side or the other so that you can move away from the pack if you feel like people are closing in on you.

- Negative split: I suggest to most people I coach that they try to do the second half of each leg of the race faster than the first half. Even if you don't end up doing that, it will help you to pace yourself so that you don't go too fast, too soon!

- Focus on the positive: Remember to be nice to yourself as your racing, and to maintain a positive attitude throughout the race.

- Pick a spot to push for the finish: You should try to keep things under control (not feel like you are going as hard as you can) until you get to a place where you know you can go really hard and still make it to the line. In some shorter races, that will be from the gun! Most of the time, it's good to pick a spot somewhere during the run, and go hard from there to the finish line.

- Run through the finish: Always run right through the finish line. All too often people slow down over the last few meters, and get caught by someone who is sprinting just behind them.

Have fun!
(I know, I keep saying that, but it's important!)

Training Programs

Some basic rules when you're setting up a training program:

1. Work at your own level – it's easy to get carried away and do too much, too soon.
2. Build in a "down week" every third or fourth week. This should be a week where you don't train as hard, or as long. In the same way that you need a full day of rest every week, you need a week that's not quite so hard every month or so to make sure that you're not overdoing things.
3. Don't forget to make time for flexibility and strength work.
4. Incorporate as many other sports and training as you can during the fall and winter. This will help you become a more rounded athlete and individual, and you will be less likely to burn out or overtrain if you're involved in other sports.

Beginner program

Beginner programs should be geared towards a summer of racing. The rest of the year should be spent involved in a variety of sports. Here are some suggestions for a program geared for a series of races in July and August, with more specific triathlon training beginning in May.

May training:

Monday	off
Tuesday	Swim: 1-2 x goal race distance, lots of drills and technique work/ Circuit training
Wednesday	Bike: Goal race distance – easy effort.
Thursday	Run: Goal race distance – easy effort/ Circuit training
Friday	Off
Saturday	Swim: 1-2 x goal race distance, lots of drills and technique work
Sunday	Bike/ Run Transition workout – Goal race distance – easy effort

June training:

Monday	off
Tuesday	Swim: 2-3 x goal race distance, lots of drills and technique work, interval sessions should emphasize distance and VO_2 work/ Circuit training
Wednesday	Bike: 1-2 x Goal race distance – easy effort.
Thursday	Run: Interval training day: sessions should emphasize VO_2 and AT work/ Circuit training
Friday	Off
Saturday	Swim: 2-3 x goal race distance, lots of drills and technique work, intervals should emphasize distance efforts/ Circuit training
Sunday	Bike/ Run Transition workout – 10 mins w'up bike; 5 mins w'up run; 2-4 x 2km bike/ 1km run; 5 mins w'down run; 10 mins w'down bike

July and August training:

Monday	off
Tuesday	Swim: 2-3 x goal race distance, less drill and technique work, interval sessions should emphasize AT and speed.
Wednesday	Bike: 1-2 x goal race distance – easy effort.
Thursday	Run: Interval training day: sessions should emphasize VO_2 and AT work
Friday	Off
Saturday	Swim: 2-3 x goal race distance, lots of drills and technique work, intervals should emphasize AT efforts
Sunday	Bike/ Run Transition workout – 10 mins w'up bike; 5 mins w'up run; 2-4 x 2km bike/ 1km run; 5 mins w'down run; 10 mins w'down bike

Every second week:

Friday	Off
Saturday	Swim: 200–600m easy; Bike: 15-20 mins easy; Run: 10 mins easy
Sunday	Race

Advanced program

Children involved in more advanced programs will likely train for more of the year. The fall and winter will likely involve competitive racing in either swimming or biking.

It is important to remember, though, that there needs to be some down time built into the schedule where training is reduced to a minimum. If you've been racing through July and August, then September should be the down month. If you're involved in a competitive cross country running program, though, that will be difficult, which means you'll be best to take that down time in November and December.

The fall (September to December) is traditionally when cross country running programs take place and when many competitive swim programs start up. Rather than try to work around that training, this is a great time to work on your swimming and running skills. If you can, though, try and fit in a couple of bike workouts each week – it will help you later in the year when you decide to incorporate more bike training into your program, and will provide a bit of a break from running and swimming.

The fall and winter are also a good time to emphasize circuit and weight training.

Fall Program:

Monday	Swim (intervals, drills and technique work with group)/ Run: Easy distance
Tuesday	Run (intervals)/ Circuit or weight training
Wednesday	Swim (intervals, drills and technique work with group)/ Bike: Easy distance
Thursday	Run (strength – hill training or longer intervals)/ Circuit or weight training
Friday	Off
Saturday	Swim (intervals, drills and technique work with group)/ Run (intervals or steady paced effort)
Sunday	Bike: Easy distance/ Circuit training

Winter Program:

During the winter more serious athletes will want to try and build in some quality training on their bikes. The swim and run programs won't change much during this time.

Monday	Swim (intervals, drills and technique work with group)/ Bike: Easy distance
Tuesday	Run (intervals)/ Circuit or weight training
Wednesday	Swim (intervals, drills and technique work with group)/ Bike: Distance, VO_2 max and AT intervals
Thursday	Run (strength – hill training or longer intervals)/ Circuit or weight training
Friday	Off
Saturday	Swim (intervals, drills and technique work with group)/ Bike: Distance and VO_2 max sessions/ Circuit training
Sunday	Run: Easy distance

Those pursuing a more competitive triathlon program in the summer should also begin to focus on triathlon training in May or June. Here are some suggestions for training for those months:

May and June Training:

Monday	Run (easy)-distance should build each week, but shouldn't exceed about 1 ½ x race distance
Tuesday	Swim (intervals) – Emphasis should be on distance and VO$_2$ max workouts
Wednesday	Bike: Emphasis should be on distance and VO$_2$ max workouts
Thursday	Swim (easy) – drills and technique should be emphasized, along with some longer aerobic intervals (100-400 m depending on age and ability.)
	Run (intervals) – Alternate weeks: First week the emphasis should be on strength type sets – hills and or stairs. The second week the emphasis should be on distance and VO$_2$ max workouts.
Friday	Off
Saturday	Swim (intervals) – Emphasis should be on distance and VO$_2$ max workouts
	Bike (distance) – distance should build each week, but shouldn't exceed about 1 ½ x race distance
Sunday	Bike/ Run Transition workout – This should start at the goal race distance, and gradually build to about 1 ½ times race distance

July and August Training:

Monday	Run (easy) – Distance should be one to 1 ½ x race distance
Tuesday	Swim (intervals) – Emphasis should be on AT and speed workouts
Wednesday	Bike: Emphasis should be on AT and speed workouts
Thursday	Swim (easy) – drills and technique should be emphasized, along with some longer aerobic intervals (100-400 m depending on age and ability.)
	Run– (intervals) – Emphasis should be on AT and speed workouts
Friday	Off
Saturday	Swim (intervals) – Emphasis should be on AT and speed workouts
	Bike (distance) – distance should build each week, but shouldn't exceed about 1 ½ x race distance
Sunday	Bike/ Run Transition workout – 10-20 mins w'up bike; 5-10 mins w'up run; 3-6 x 2km bike/ 1km run; 5-10 mins w'down run; 10-20 mins w'down bike

Every second week:

Friday	Off
Saturday	Swim: 600- 1,000 m easy; Bike: 20 mins easy; Run: 10-20 mins easy
Sunday	Race

APPENDIX:
Canadian and
US standards

Triathlon Canada follows these guidelines for junior racing in Canada.

Age-appropriate race distances

Age Division	12 to 13	14 to 15	16 to 19
Maximum Distances	300m / 15km / 3km	500m / 15km / 4km	750m / 20km / 5km

Age-appropriate equipment

Age Division	12 to 13	14 to 15	16 to 18
Triathlon Bars (Aero Bars)	No	Yes	Yes
Clipless Pedals & Cycling Shoes	No	Yes	Yes
Gear Ratios (Recommended)	45 x 16	52 x 16	52 x 16
Race Wheels	No	Yes	Yes

Junior Racers

Once these athletes turn 16, they have a choice to enter "drafting" races or to remain in non-drafting events. For the non-drafting races the athletes can enter any Kids of Steel or Adult race they want.

"Drafting" races require a different approach and have different rules. Junior (ages 16 to 19 as of December 31) athletes who wish to participate in "draft legal" races must:

1 Have their entry confirmed in writing by their Provincial Governing Body (PGB);
2 Have completed a drafting clinic approved by their PGB; and their bike must comply with the applicable Triathlon Canada Rules – see below.

E.3.1 Bicycles

Bicycles must have the following characteristics:

a) For **elite and junior competition categories** in standard distance duathlon and triathlon events, the frame of the bicycle shall be of a traditional pattern, i.e., built around a main triangle of three straight or tapered tubular elements which may be round, oval, flattened, teardrop shaped or otherwise in cross-section.

b) For **elite and junior competitions** in standard distance duathlons and triathlons, BOTH wheels must be of spoke construction. In long distances or age group competition, covers are allowed on the rear wheel, however this provision may be changed by the Technical Director in the interest of safety, i.e., high-winds.

c) The frame will be no more that two (2) meters long, and fifty (50) centimeters wide for **elite and juniors**, in Triathlon National Cup Series, Duathlon National Cup Series, Triathlon and Duathlon National Championships. For all other competition, two (2) meters long and seventy-five (75) centimeters wide will be permitted.

d) The frame will measure at least 24 centimeters from the ground to the center of the chain wheel axle.

e) A vertical line touching the front-most point of the saddle will be no more than 5 centimeters in front of and no more than 15 centimeters behind a vertical line passing through the center of the chain wheel axle. A competitor must not have the capability of adjusting the saddle beyond these lines during competition.

f) There will be no fewer than 54 centimeters and no more than 65 centimeters between a vertical line passing through the center of the chain wheel axle and a vertical line through the center of the front wheel axle. (Exceptions may be given for the bicycles of very tall or very short competitors).

g) Farings, which reduce air resistance, are prohibited.

h) No wheel may contain mechanisms which are capable of accelerating it.

i) Handlebar ends must be plugged, tires well glued, headsets tight and wheels true.

j) There must be a brake on each wheel.

k) Non-traditional or unusual bicycles or equipment shall be illegal unless prior approval has been received from the Chief Race Official prior to the start of the competition.

Rationale provided by Triathlon Canada for the above rules:

Rule Description	Rationale	Age Groups Affected
Aero bars are not permitted	• Balance, bike handling and coordination are critical skills to develop in the initial years of training cycling. If aero bars are introduced prior to the mastery of these skills – balance in particular – the athlete can put themselves and others at risk of accident. • Aero bars also restrict maneuverability and responsiveness while on the bike.	12 / 13
Aero bars must be draft-legal and comply with ITU standards.	• Draft-legal aero bars are more stable than traditional aero bars. • Draft-legal aero bars are designed to be safer in case of collisions or accidental falls. • If athletes wish to pursue higher levels of the sport, they must use draft-legal bars. Earlier exposure to draft-legal aero bars will facilitate skill acquisition.	14 / 15 16 / 19

Rule Description	Rationale	Age Groups Affected
Clipless pedals are not permitted.	• Clipless pedal systems are unstable for walking and running; they pose significant risk of injury while traveling in and out of transition *(e.g. slipping/tripping on clips; falling/toppling while trying to "clip in"; colliding/sliding into other athletes and/or bikes)* • Clipless pedal systems also lock feet into pedals, thus increasing the chance of injury *(unless fit properly)*.	12 / 13
The exception to the clipless pedal restriction is: wide-based platform pedals *(for mountain bikes)* **designed with a shoe cleat that can be used with running shoes.**	Running shoes can be used on wide-based pedals, therefore reducing the risk associated with traveling (walking/running) in traditional cycling shoes with protruding clips (running/walking).	All age groups.

Rule Description	Rationale	Age Groups Affected
Race wheels are not permitted.	• Race wheels with (<24) spokes pose a serious danger to athletes who may accidentally step into a wheel or trip over a bike *(e.g. in transition; after a collision/crash).* This situation has caused serious injuries at the elite level. • Race wheels are also lighter and more "flighty" than regular wheels, putting athletes at risk for "blow-overs" (in the wind).	12 / 13

Standards for the United States:

USA Triathlon recommends the following race distances for each age group:

11-12, 13-15: 200m swim/10k bike/2k run

Youth Elite

The Youth Elite division is for athletes 13-15 years old who have a little more experience and enjoy the Elite ITU "draft-legal" style of racing. The distances are slightly longer (400m swim/10k bike/2.5k run) and because of close competition, the bicycle leg allows drafting among competitors.

Junior

At most local and regional USAT-sanctioned races of short and intermediate distances, there is a 15-19 age group and a 20-24 age group, along with all the older adult age groups. The "Junior Elite" division exists at most ITU-Style races, such as the USAT National Championships and ITU World Championships in the USAT National Athlete Development ITU-Style Race Series. In ITU-Style races, the divisions begin with Youth Elite (ages 13-15), competing in a super-sprint distance (400m swim/10K bike/2.5K run). At National and International competitions, the Junior division includes athletes aged 16-19 who race the sprint distance (750m swim/20k bike/5k run). The athlete's age on December 31 of the year of competition is the athlete's "racing age" all year long.

USA Triathlon recommends that Junior athletes (ages16-19) should compete in sprint distance (750m/20K/5K) races, while those ages18-23 may compete in sprint distance or triathlon/intermediate distance (1.5K/40K/10K). USA Triathlon does not recommend that athletes under age 20 compete in events longer than 1.5k swim/40k bike/10k run.

Junior Elite National and World Championships

Athletes who compete in USAT National Championships and ITU World Championships contend for the highest honors in the sport. Junior and U23 athletes who race in ITU-style events strive to be their very best and eventually even represent the USA in International competition including the Olympic Games. For this reason, all Junior and U23 national and world championships are now in the ITU-style format to prepare athletes for future elite competition.

Photo & Illustration Credits